HIRED!

100 INTERVIEW QUESTIONS PLUS 50 MUST-READ TIPS FOR TODAY'S JOB MARKET

MATTHEW BRIGGSON

Matthew Briggson

Table of Contents

INTRODUCTION

INTERVIEWS ARE AN ANAMOLY

When we consider the variables that have the most significant impact on opportunities and success throughout one's career, the interview process sticks out as an anomaly. Education, experience, networking, and performance all take a significant investment of time and money, and while these factors all hold a strong influence, the ramifications of success or failure during a two-hour interview are unmatched.

I'm going to let you in on a secret that may be either convenient or inconvenient for you: The most qualified candidate on paper will usually not receive the offer letter. This means that the person who outperformed the other candidates over many years, sometimes decades, will most likely walk away empty handed while the candidate who outperforms the other candidates over the course of a two-hour event will receive the job offer. The good news is, you can use this information to your advantage. If you are the most qualified candidate heading into the interview process, this book can show you how to sustain that advantage across the finish line. If you are not the most qualified candidate on paper, this book can help you leap frog the other candidates and win when it matters most. The problem is that you likely will not know where you stand against the other candidates, so you should always be prepared to hit a home run during the interview.

Introduction

I was likely the most qualified candidate heading into my first professional interview. I had a very high GPA, was involved in extracurricular activities, and had highly relevant experience. My interview did not go as planned. To be blunt, it was a complete and utter disaster. Heading into the interview, I thought I was prepared. I researched the company's website, was ready to discuss my resume inside and out, and even had a few questions prepared for the interviewer. Once the interview got started, I quickly realized that my perception of being "prepared" was far from reality. The problem was not that I was lazy in my preparation, it was that I prepared in all the wrong ways.

Looking back, I am glad my first interview turned out so poorly. If it had just been mediocre, I likely would have kept applying the same techniques over and over until I settled into a less than desirable job. Because the interview was such a disaster, I decided that I would do everything in my power to never let that happen again. This lead me down a path of research which included discussions with seasoned interviewers and hiring managers in multiple industries. I did not want to get caught up in what "interview experts" on the internet said. Instead, I wanted to go directly to the sources to find out what interviewers look for when hiring a candidate.

My dedication paid off as I landed my dream job early on in my career, but my interest and intrigue in the interview process never went away. I continued my research and discussions with hiring managers and used it to my advantage in subsequent interviews as I progressed through my career. Now as a business owner, I sit on the other side of the interview desk and know what to look for when hiring vendors, contractors, and employees. This book is a culmination of my research as well as my experience on both sides of the interview desk.

The book has two main sections. The first section consists of 50 interview tips which are broken out by actions you can take before, during, and after the interview as well as tips on preparing for interview questions and utilizing effective body language techniques. If 50 action items make you feel overwhelmed, don't be. A few tips may take some time but most of them are either best practices that will not take any additional preparation time or simple actions that take less than 15 minutes.

The second section consists of 100 wide-ranging interview questions and example responses. Each question includes an analysis on why the interviewer is asking the question and what they are looking for out of the response from the candidate. Additionally, every question includes a section on what to specifically avoid in your response to the interviewer. In reality, you will likely only receive about 10 questions during each interview session, but I want you to be confident in answering any question that comes your way.

Similar to the 50 interview tips, it might seem overwhelming to study 100 interview questions and formulate your own word-for-word responses. However, the questions are presented in a way to encourage the reader to take a holistic approach to the interview process. Attempting to memorize your own responses to 100 interview questions would not only be a painfully tedious process, it would also be a recipe for disaster when the interview rolls around. This book is set up for you to understand the "why" behind each interview question and then get you thinking as you read the example responses. Once you understand the real meaning behind the questions, you will realize you do not need to memorize answers. Instead, you will be able to spend your preparation time bullet pointing information about your personality, experience, and background that will equip you to answer any question that comes your way during the interview.

This book also includes an appendix on virtual and phone interviews. In today's environment, these interviews are becoming much more common and are often used to screen candidates before a more formal interview takes place. Even though most of the preparation fundamentals are the same as an in-person interview, there are some unique considerations you should be aware of to set yourself up for success.

Before we get started, I want to offer you a few words of encouragement. Knowing how to ace interviews does not happen over the course of a couple hours. It will require a commitment, but I can promise you that the end result will be well worth it. If you have an interview coming up and already feel overwhelmed, do not get discouraged. It is critical to maintain a positive mindset and persevere. I would recommend developing a plan and schedule in advance to get through the information in this book, while leaving yourself some time to practice. Most importantly, believe in yourself and great things will happen!

Note for Urgent Situations

Is your interview only a couple days out or maybe even tomorrow? I have been in your situation and I know how it can feel helpless to be faced with so much information to cover, in so little time. If you are crunched for time, you can still get a lot of value out of this book, but I would encourage you to focus your limited time on a couple key areas. I recommend reading and taking action on the tips that have an asterisk (*) next to them. These tips can be executed in a limited amount of time and can be extremely beneficial to your interview success, even if it is only a day or two away. I also recommend trying to get through interview questions #1-#20 (the more the better) and leave yourself a couple hours to bullet point your own responses and practice out loud.

PART I: 50 INTERVIEW TIPS

BEFORE THE INTERVIEW

1. RESEARCH THE BACKGROUNDS OF THE INTERVIEWERS*

The company you are interviewing with will typically send over the interview schedule in advance. If there are multiple rounds of interviews, you may only interview with one person the first round and then with multiple people in subsequent rounds.

It is essential to know some background details about each person who interviews you. Each interview usually begins with small talk to break the ice. Having knowledge of the interviewer's professional background goes a long way in building early rapport. It is also an excellent way to develop relevant questions for the interviewer at the end of the session (See tip #2 for more detail).

I recommend starting your research with the company's website. If it is a small to mid-size company, you will usually come across profiles of the leadership team. Larger companies do not always publish leadership profiles. If you are unable to find the profile of your interviewer on the company's site, LinkedIn will be an excellent resource. Within each LinkedIn profile, you will find "Experience," "Skills & Endorsements," and "Activity" which will include articles or posts made by that individual to their network. There is also an "Interests" section which will show which companies and organizations that person is connected to. Reviewing the interests section is a great way to find clues about which causes and charities they focus on outside of work. I do not recommend making a "Connect" request to your interviewers on LinkedIn before the interview. They may not recognize who you are beforehand, and it is a much more natural progression to make the request after meeting them during the interview.

You can also conduct a Google search to look for articles and information on your interviewer. You will often find local news articles about business leaders getting involved in community and charitable events.

As you are conducting research on your interviewers, jot down bullet points of relevant information that you can leverage during your interview. Here is an example of what your notes might look like:

Jim Vandenberg, Director of Procurement

- *Attended University of Michigan (From the dates, I'm noting that he attended when they won the 1997 national championship in football).*
- *Manages a team of 21 professionals responsible for sourcing raw materials, warehousing, suppliers, and logistics.*
- *Started career in corporate finance.*
- *Interested in St. Jude's Children hospital.*

Possessing this background information on Jim gives you a huge advantage for the interview! The key is not to lead with any of this information but to naturally incorporate it into your conversation and leverage it to ask excellent questions. For example, you would never want to say something like:

"I saw that you were attending Michigan in 1997, did you attend any games the year the football team won the championship?"

Or

"I noted that you follow St. Jude's Hospital. What other charitable organizations interest you?"

These questions would be coming out of left field and scream to the interviewer that you investigated them. Instead, use this information during the natural progression of the conversation. For example, the interviewer will typically tell you some of their background information in the beginning. If the interview is still in the "small talk" phase and Jim stated that he attended the University of Michigan, you can say something like:

"I'm always thrilled when fall comes along and it's time for college football season. Michigan has such a rich history in football. Did they have good teams while you attended?"

You can be assured that 99 out of 100 times, Jim is going to light up like a Christmas tree and tell you about being on campus when they won the national championship. This will get him excited to discuss it with you and the interview starts out in a positive direction. If football (or whatever background information you found on the interviewer) is not your thing, do not sweat it. You certainly do not want to use the above example if you have no interest in football. However, you should be able to find something else in their background that you can relate to and bring it up when the time is right.

At the end of the interview Jim is going to ask if you have any questions. Since you researched his background information, you can ask him some excellent questions you come up with in advance such as:

"As the director of procurement, how do you take steps to mitigate the risk of large or unexpected price movements in raw materials?"

"Does XYZ Company offer employees the opportunity to get exposure working with multiple departments?"

"Does XYZ Company encourage employees to give back through charitable causes?"

Notice how each question is driven by background information from the notes above? They are also highly relevant questions that Jim will be eager to discuss.

You can certainly come to the interview with relevant questions that are not rooted in an interviewer's background information, but most candidates struggle to come up with two or three strong questions for each interviewer. Leveraging their background information is an excellent way to formulate them.

2. DEVELOP QUESTIONS FOR EACH INTERVIEWER*

One of the most critical parts of the interview is towards the end when the interviewer will ask you if you have any questions for them. Not only do they expect you to ask questions, they also expect the questions to show that you did your research on the company and are genuinely excited about the position.

Candidates should be ready to ask each interviewer a minimum of 2 questions, but I always recommend having 3 questions prepared. When coming up with your questions, be sure to avoid any question that can be answered with a simple "yes" or "no" response. For example:

"Does XYZ Company offer paid leave for new fathers?"

Even though this question will probably not result in the interviewer providing a simple "yes" or "no," it is possible to be answered with a one-word response and is usually not relevant to the interview. In fact, the interviewer may not even know the answer to this question which would disrupt the flow of the conversation. This type of question should be saved for your HR contact after they offer you the job.

Your questions should be broad enough to get the interviewer thinking but specific enough to their background and role that they are enthusiastic about answering them. This is too broad of a question:

"What do employees enjoy about working at XYZ Company?"

Instead be more specific to the interviewer's role and show you did some research with this question:

"As someone who works closely with a wide range of customers in the consumer products industry, where do you look for opportunities to bring added value to your customers?"

The best way to develop highly relevant questions for each interviewer is to research their background and experience (see tip 1). Below are a couple more examples of taking notes on your research to create high quality questions.

Nicole Bennet, Accounting Manager

- *Attended University of Utah, was in Beta Alpha Psi (accounting group).*
- *Spent time in public accounting at a Big Four Firm (PwC).*
- *Is responsible for overseeing quarterly and annual financial reporting with SEC and coordination of audit with independent accounting firm.*
- *Interested in hiking and outdoors groups.*

Question 1: "What role does technology have on the challenges and opportunities facing the financial reporting profession as it relates to SEC reporting?"

Question 2: "How do you leverage student organizations on college campuses in your recruiting efforts?"

Question 3: "How does XYZ Company encourage employees to be active and participate in fitness activities?"

Kelvin Smith, Regional Sales Manager Software company

- *Lives in Chicago, responsible for all Midwest sales.*
- *Previously was a recruiter for sales positions.*
- *Oversees large sales team with customers primarily in automotive manufacturing.*
- *Interested in Veteran Affairs and supporting VA hospitals.*

Question 1: "How does your team leverage CRM (customer relationship management) technology to bring value to your customers?"

Question 2: "With software and technology changing so rapidly, how does your sales team work with the operations and technology teams to leverage customer feedback and interaction?"

Question 3: "How does XYZ Company and its employees give back to charities, veterans causes, and the local community?"

It can be challenging to remember all of your questions if you will be interviewing with multiple people. Be sure to jot them down under the name of each interviewer and bring them with you. You will typically have a brief break between interviews which will afford you the time to review them. You should usually avoid glancing down at them during the interview but just having them there will aid your confidence.

3. ASK THE INTERVIEW CONTACT WHAT TYPE OF INTERVIEW TO EXPECT

The style of the interview is dependent on the company's preference. Most companies prefer a traditional style interview where the candidate meets individually with the interviewers in separate sessions. However, some companies will conduct other types of interviews including:

*Panel interviews where multiple people observe the interview session and take turns asking the candidate questions.

*Presentation interviews where the candidate is expected to put together a presentation and present it to a group of interviewers.

*Brain teasers or test type interviews where the candidate has a fixed amount of time to complete a competency test to assess knowledge and critical thinking skills.

Some interviews are set up as a combination of the types listed above. For example, the candidate may be asked to complete a 30-minute competency test before commencing a more traditional one-on-one interview session. Regardless of the type of interview coming your way, you can be fully prepared to succeed. However, it is essential to know what type of interview to prepare for as soon as possible.

The type of interview can usually be determined by the schedule or itinerary sent over. If the company does expect you to give a presentation, they will let you know up-front. If the schedule shows you meeting with various individuals in interview sessions, you can expect to have a more traditional style interview. If your schedule only shows the beginning and end times of the interview, be sure to reach out to your contact and ask them what to expect. Being mentally prepared for one-on-one interview sessions is much different than interviewing in front of a multi-person panel. When asking what to expect, be sure not to phrase it in a way that insinuates you are looking for tips or inside information about the process. Instead, emphasize that you would like to know what to expect to help you prepare for the interview. Here is an example email you could use to send to your HR contact:

"Hi (first name),

I am looking forward to interviewing with XYZ Company on mm/dd (date). As I am starting to prepare for the interview, I wanted to reach out to you with a few questions that came up.

Should I expect the interview to be conducted in multiple sessions or will I be interviewing in front of a panel of people?

If possible, could you please provide me with the names of the people who will be included in the interview process?

Should I bring a calculator or pencils for any testing procedures?

Once again, I greatly appreciate the opportunity to interview with XYZ.

Thank you,
(your first name)

4. TAKE NOTE OF THE COMPANY'S "ABOUT US" INFORMATION

Companies will almost always have a section on their website that discusses their values, culture, mission statement, history, and objectives. By absorbing this information, you will have a great sense of what they tend to look for in candidates. Many studies show that companies place a higher emphasis on cultural fit than any other trait when deciding whether to hire a candidate.

It is not uncommon for an interviewer to test a candidate on their knowledge of the company's values. They may ask the candidate which values they look for in an employer to see how well they align with the company's values. You can use the information obtained in your research to emphasize key values of your own that match up well with those of the company.

I do want to emphasize that you should not waste time memorizing everything on the company's "about us" section. It is more important to take bullet point notes of their values, mission, and culture. You can use that information to think of ways to emphasize your own values and interests that closely align with those of the company. If a company's values include the following terms:

*Integrity

*Accountability

*Diversity

*Quality

You should find ways to integrate some of these values into your answers to the interview questions. For example, if the interviewer asks you to provide them with an example of a time you faced a tight deadline on a project and in part of your answer you say, "I always place a high emphasis on quality, no matter what type of pressure I face," you have successfully aligned your answer with one of the company's values and the interviewer will usually make that connection.

5. USE TWITTER/FACEBOOK/LINKEDIN TO RESEARCH THE COMPANY'S PERSONALITY

Social media is an excellent way to learn about the culture and atmosphere within a company. Companies will usually post news articles, press releases, updates, and engage with their audience on their social media page. Reviewing this activity on social media will give you a strong sense of their culture and tone. Is the tone they use on their social media pages very professional or is it more laid back and casual? Do they only self-promote on their pages or do they find other ways to engage with their audience? What positive news and information are they sharing with their audience?

Within a few minutes of reviewing their social media activity, you will get a strong sense of the company's culture and personality. This will usually be an indicator of the style of the interview. It may be serious and professional or more laid back and casual. You will not know for sure until the interview takes place but their activity on social media will provide a lot of clues. If any exciting updates or news articles shared by the company catch your attention, be sure to take note of them and you can bring them up during the small talk phase of the interview or even turn them into a question for the interviewer.

6. IF PUBLICLY TRADED, RESEARCH THE BUSINESS AND MD&A SECTIONS OF THE LATEST 10-K*

If the company is publicly traded, they are required to file an annual report with the SEC (Securities and Exchange Commission) which is then made available to the public. The report provides a wealth of information on the Company including its history, business operations, risks, and financial health.

To find out whether a company is publicly traded, you can go to Google Finance and search for their name. If they come up with an actively traded stock, they are a public company. You can then go over to SEC.gov and click on "Company Filings" in the upper right-hand corner. Then you can search for the company by name or stock ticker symbol and it will bring up a history of their filings. Next look for the "10-K" filing with the most recent date and click on "Documents" and then the link to the document on the next page.

You should see a large 10-K document appear in your browser. Often this document can be over 100 pages but don't feel overwhelmed as we are just going to focus on a couple of key areas within the document. The first section to review is the "Business" section which can be found under "Part 1" and "Item 1." There should be a clickable link titled "Business" which will take you directly to the section.

The business section will provide you an overview and history of the company. It will also delve into the company's products or services, brands, segments, investments, industry, and risk factors. The type of information found in the business section is deemed important enough by the SEC and company to disclose to current and potential investors to aid in their decision making. I recommend either reading through this section and taking detailed notes or printing the section out (be careful not to print the whole 10-K!) and highlighting key areas.

I also recommend doing the same with the MD&A (management's discussion and analysis of financial condition and results of operations) section within the 10-K. This section provides management commentary about the financial results of the company. If sales increased by 50% in a product category in the current year, this is the section that will tell the reader the drivers behind the change. Even if you are not interviewing for a financial position, having knowledge of the company's financial performance will be valuable during the interview process. You will get a sense of where the company is performing well and where they are experiencing challenges.

Discussing information from these sections will demonstrate to the interviewers that you did your homework on the company. You can use this information to develop questions about the company although try not to get too specific (avoid "What new products contributed to the 5% increase in sales in Europe last year?") and focus on the positives (avoid "What do you think will be the outcome of the $100 million-dollar lawsuit against the company?"). A good question from the business section of the 10-K might be:

"I noted that XZY Company introduced three new product lines last year (names of product lines). Can you discuss some of the ways XYZ company places a high priority on product innovation?"

If the company is not publicly traded, you can still gather valuable information using their own website (tip 4), social media (tip 5), Wikipedia, and Google.

7. CREATE OR CLEAN UP YOUR LINKEDIN ACCOUNT

Many studies have shown that up to 90% of hiring mangers use LinkedIn to vet job candidates. If you have an incomplete LinkedIn profile or no profile at all, it can raise some red flags. Ideally, your LinkedIn profile is in great shape before you even apply for any position. If your LinkedIn profile has not been created or needs a facelift, be sure to update it ASAP in the interview process. Below are some tips for optimizing your LinkedIn profile:

*Use a high-quality professional looking picture for your image. If you do not have one, put on professional clothing, find a non-distracting background and have someone take your picture for you. If you have the budget, you could hire a photographer to take a professional picture.

*Use a professional headline such as: "Account Executive in the Software Industry at XYZ Company" or "International Business Major Graduating in May 2018 seeking a Full-Time Opportunity."

*Brand your profile with a professional background photo. You can use Google to search for LinkedIn profile background images. They should be roughly 1400x425 pixels.

*Spell check your profile in full detail and then have a friend or family member who pays attention to detail spell check it for you. Spelling and grammar errors can be devastating to your brand if they are observed by the interviewer.

*Ensure your educational and professional experience sections are accurate and up-to-date. Try to fill in any gaps of time if possible.

*List your skills and ask your friends and network for endorsements.

*Target a minimum of 100 connections. If you already connected with your friends and family, reach out and make connections with people who have something in common with your industry, education, location, interests, etc. You can even highlight this commonality when you make the connection request. Do not be afraid to put yourself out there and build up your connections to a respectable level.

*Share news articles or even write a LinkedIn post yourself. Those checking out your profile will see what you have shared with your network in your activity section. This is a great opportunity to show knowledge and enthusiasm for your industry by sharing news or writing a LinkedIn post.

*Connect with groups or organizations on LinkedIn. Just about every industry and profession will have many groups you can connect with. If you perform a search on your industry (example: "accounting"), tons of groups will pop up and you can join or follow them.

8. REACH OUT TO AN EMPLOYEE OF THE COMPANY BEFORE THE INTERVIEW (NOT THE INTERVIEWERS)

Connecting with an employee at the company before the interview is an excellent way to learn more about the environment and culture. If you have a connection through family or friends, you can ask them if they will make the introduction and then set up a call or time to grab coffee. If you do not have a personal connection to someone who works at the company, LinkedIn will be your best friend.

The purpose of this connection is to gain a better understanding of the company, not to appear as though you are looking for insider information about the interview. It would be a bad idea to try to connect with any of the interviewers or anyone associated with the interview process. I would even take it a step further and avoid connecting with anyone in the department you are interviewing with as they will likely have direct interaction with someone who will be part of the interview process. If the company is less than 25 employees, I would avoid this tip all together since everyone will be closely connected.

If you end up using LinkedIn to make the connection, you can search for the company name and look for an individual who shares something in common with you. They may have attended the same college, share a mutual LinkedIn connection, or even simply live in the same city. Ideally, you will connect with an employee who is somewhat new to the company (below the manager level) and use a connection request message such as "Hi (first name), I noted we both attended Florida State University and I recently applied for a position at (company name). I wanted to connect with someone who has some experience working there."

After you become connected, you can either send them a LinkedIn email or better yet, ask them if they would be available for a 10-minute call. An example message could be:

"Hi (first name),

Thanks for accepting my connection. I am interested in learning more about the culture at (company name) and what it takes to succeed there. Are you available for a quick 10-minute call in the coming days?

Thank you!"

Be prepared to take notes on your call and listen to anything they are willing to share. Be sure to keep your own questions high level and do not pry for information related to the interviewers or interview process. Typically, they will be more than happy to share information about the company that can be very valuable to your preparation.

9. SIGNUP FOR GOOGLE ALERTS

Google Alerts finds news and events on any search term and sends an email to you when that news is posted to the internet. Google Alerts lets you decide how often you would like to receive notifications to your email inbox and enables you to select the source of the information (news, blogs, videos, discussion pages, etc.).

I recommend setting up Google Alerts on the industry in general and on the Company where you will interview. For example, if you are an accountant, I would set up an alert for "accounting" and for "XYZ Company." If something newsworthy occurs before the interview, you will be notified right away.

Consider this scenario: A supply chain analyst named Allison interviewed at a large consumer products company in their supply chain department. Allison had already gone through one round of interviews with the company and was well prepared and optimistic about the prospects of landing the position. When she arrived for the second interview, she quickly noticed that everyone who spoke to her seemed anxious and quiet – much different than their personalities in her first round of interviews. Allison eventually concluded that their lackluster tone around her indicated they had already made the decision not to hire her. She started to question her prior optimism and the interview did not go anything like the first one. Finally, the last interviewer mentioned to her

"I bet you can imagine how chaotic it has been around the plant in the past 48 hours."

Allison had no idea what he was talking about. When she got home she Googled the company and found multiple news headlines announcing the company had a $50 million-dollar product recall a few days prior. Had Allison been aware of this recall going into the interview, she would have known why the employees seemed on edge. She also could have used this information to express her sympathies to the employees as they were under immense stress. Always be informed. Signing up for Google Alerts will ensure you avoid this type of situation.

10. CLEANUP YOUR SOCIAL MEDIA ACCOUNTS

According to a recent CareerBuilder survey, 70% of companies review a candidate's social media accounts as part of their decision-making process. If you have Facebook, Twitter, or another social media account, your potential employer is not only likely to review it but also factor it into their decision whether to hire you. Below are some tips to implement to ensure you will not be hurt by your social media accounts.

*Choose a respectable looking photo for your image.

*Delete your political or controversial posts. Remember, in today's world it does not take much for something to be deemed "offensive."

*Delete or un-tag yourself from photos that depict excessive drinking, drug use, sexual connotations, or anything else illegal or questionable.

*Update your privacy settings so only approved contacts and friends can view your profile details.

*Add some fresh new content to your social media accounts. Post or tweet interesting articles related to your profession.

11. PRINT OFF EXTRA COPIES OF YOUR RESUME ON HIGH QUALITY PAPER

A good rule of thumb is to determine how many people will be interviewing you and multiply that number by two to determine the number of resume copies to bring to the interview. You never want to be in a situation where someone at the company asks for a copy of your resume and you cannot provide it because you ran out of copies. You may end up conversing with individuals at the company who do not interview you but request a copy of your resume.

Resumes should be printed off on high quality paper that is slightly thicker than the average standard printer paper. Most printers and copiers use 20 lb. paper while resume paper should be at least 24 lb. sheets. There is no need to spend a fortune on your resume paper.

12. PLAN TO BRING A PROFESSIONAL PORTFOLIO WITH A NOTE PAD AND PEN

I'm a big fan of the plain manila office folders. You probably know the which ones I'm referring to. They cost $5 for about 100 of them. However, they simply do not cut it for an interview. You will want to bring a professional looking binder to hold your resumes, business cards (see tip 13), and notepad and pen for taking notes. With many options out there, be sure to choose one that is conservative in nature (avoid bright colors and images on the outside).

I typically recommend portfolios with a dark black leather look to them.

Be sure to include plenty of resume copies, business cards, a notebook, a few pens/pencils, and any notes you plan to bring to the interview. It can be tempting to unload your whole wallet or purse into a portfolio but just remember that the interviewer will have a firsthand view so make sure it looks clean and organized.

13. BRING BUSINESS CARDS, EVEN IF YOU ARE NOT CURRENTLY EMPLOYED

Each interviewer will typically hand you a business card when you first meet. Always remember to bring your own business cards so you can reciprocate and hand one back. Similar to the rule of thumb for the number of resumes, multiply the number of interviewers you expect by two and bring at least that many business cards. You may end up exchanging business cards with other employees of the company who introduce themselves. You never want to make it difficult for someone at the company to contact you.

Just graduating school or not currently employed? No worries, you should still create a personal business card. In fact, even if you are employed by another company, I still recommend creating a personal business card. You do not want a potential employer contacting you through your work email address or, even worse, your work phone number.

Your personal business card does not need to be fancy. It does not need a logo or eccentric colors. Just be sure it looks professional and includes your name, personal email address, and phone number. If you do have experience in a professional position and you are applying for a similar position, you can include a title such as "Account Executive" or "Financial Analyst" but in most cases, it is not necessary to include a title.

14. BRING REFERENCES TO THE INTERVIEW

I typically do not recommend listing the contact information of references directly on your resume. Some choose to list a section at the bottom for references that says, "Available Upon Request." This method is not necessarily a bad idea, but it is already implied that all candidates have references. As such it is okay to leave off the references section altogether on your resume. Keep in mind that if you say references are "Available Upon Request" on your resume, they need to be available during the interview. I have heard too many stories about candidates who state this on their resume but when the interviewer asks them for the references, they freeze like a deer in the headlights. The interviewer will likely perceive this as insincere and it will hurt your chances for a job offer.

The references document should be separate from the resume but have the same resume heading that includes your name and contact information. The references document should be printed on the same high-quality paper as the resume (see tip 11) and you should bring the same number of copies as your resume.

I recommend listing three references who are associated with your professional experience, work history, or educational background. Always pick references who will speak highly of you and ask them for their permission in advance.

15. MAP THE DISTANCE TO YOUR INTERVIEW AND CONSIDER THE IMPACT OF TRAFFIC

Being late for an interview is a cardinal sin. Even if you knock the interview out of the park, it is almost impossible to make the interviewer forget you were late which means they would be very unlikely to extend you an offer.

This tip sounds obvious but too many candidates simply hop on to Google Maps to estimate their drive time with no regard to the time of day they will be driving or possible construction on the date of the interview. Rush hour traffic or road construction can double the estimated drive time. To avoid this costly mistake, time yourself on a practice drive during the same time of day you will be driving on the day of the interview. You should always add at least an extra 5 minutes of contingency time onto your practice drive time for unexpected circumstances on the day of the interview. If you end up arriving too early, you can park somewhere close to the vicinity for a few minutes before continuing into the company's lot. Be sure to monitor your local city websites for unexpected construction and ensure your car is gassed up and running well before the day of the interview.

It is always wise to have an emergency backup plan. If you have not done so already, I recommend downloading the Uber or

Lyft app on your phone to be prepared to use it if your car unexpectedly fails you on your drive to the interview.

16. PLAN ON BUSINESS PROFESSIONAL ATTIRE*

Unless your interview contact explicitly states otherwise, plan to dress in business professional attire. For men, this means a full matching suit with a collared shirt and tie along with matching dress shoes. For women, this is a black skirt at or below the knee with a matching suit top and blouse or a professional matching pant suit. If you are on a budget or just prefer not to take your attire to the dry cleaners, be sure to inspect it for stains and iron out the wrinkles.

Most of us can relate to clothes not fitting like they did the last time we wore them. I've heard too many stories about candidates picking out the perfect interview outfit from their closet only to find out it fits way too small or large the morning of the interview. Always try on your attire a few days in advance to ensure it fits properly.

Aside from your attire, tattoos should be covered up and jewelry should be kept simple and conservative. Be sure to schedule a haircut if necessary, shave, and trim your finger nails in advance.

I always recommend placing an umbrella in your vehicle the day before the interview, even if the weather forecast shows a 0% chance of rain. The nightmare scenario is walking into the interview drenched by a surprise rainstorm that arrived just in time for your long walk across the parking lot. You can eliminate this risk by being prepared.

17. CLEAN YOUR CAR, INSIDE AND OUT

Life can get chaotic and our vehicles often bear the brunt of always being on-the-go. If you have treated the inside of your car like an extra closet, or even worse, a trash bin, be sure to clean everything out and vacuum it before the interview.

Is it necessary to get your car detailed before the interview? Not at all. Just know that employees are constantly walking to and from the commuter parking lot. The last thing you want is for your interviewer to see a tornado of junk piled up in your vehicle. This could be perceived as a negative reflection of your own organization skills.

If you drive a $4,000 car, there is no need to go out and rent a luxury sedan. I would not advise showing up in a complete clunker, but the image is more about how you maintain your vehicle. Be sure the inside is clutter-free and relatively clean and splurge $5-$10 for a car wash.

18. PLAN TO TAKE THE MORNING OFF ON THE DAY OF THE INTERVIEW

Even if your interview is not until the afternoon, it can be beneficial to take that morning off from your current job.

Instead of worrying about getting to your interview on time, you should be focused on the interview itself.

If you cannot take the whole day off, try your best to free up two or three hours before your interview. Being rushed to your interview will add a layer of unnecessary and detrimental stress.

19. GET GOOD SLEEP THE NIGHT BEFORE THE INTERVIEW

The difference between being well rested and groggy can have a drastic impact on your interview performance. It can be difficult to sleep well the evening before a significant event. An effective way to fall asleep on time is to take time for an extra-long and strenuous workout in the afternoon or early evening. If you typically jog two miles for exercise, jog four. If you typically do three sets at the gym, do six. An extra hard workout will clear your mind and tire your body out which will usually help you fall and stay asleep. Below are a few more tips to help you arrive to the interview well rested.

*Avoid drinking alcohol or caffeine the day before the interview.

*Avoid a heavy dinner the evening prior to the interview.

*Avoid sugar and other simple carbohydrates the day before the interview.

*Drink plenty of water the day before and morning of the interview.

20. EAT BREAKFAST AND DRINK WATER THE MORNING OF THE INTERVIEW*

Not a big fan of eating breakfast? Think of the interview as a physical event. Even though you will be dressed in business attire, you will be expending a lot of energy. The average person will burn around 50 calories an hour just talking. Some interviews can last for up to four hours with you speaking the majority of the time. If you come in with an empty stomach, your body will be short on fuel and you can start to feel light headed and tired which will impact your mental clarity and performance.

At a minimum try to eat some fruit and consume some brain food such as eggs or whole wheat toast. As noted in tip 19, be sure to consume plenty of water the day before and day of the interview.

21. ARRIVE TO THE INTERVIEW LOCATION 15 MINUTES EARLY*

How early should you walk into the location of your interview? 10-15 minutes prior to the interview is usually early enough to check in with the receptionist and get situated in an office or conference room where your interview will take place. I recommend planning to be in the parking lot 15 minutes early to leave yourself 5 minutes to relax in your car, get in the right mindset (see tip 22), and make the walk to the entrance.

Keep in mind that walking in earlier than 10-15 minutes prior to the interview can make you appear over-eager and desperate. It can also be an inconvenience for the interviewer if they are preoccupied with other work or another meeting.

22. GET IN THE RIGHT MINDSET BEFORE ENTERING FOR THE INTERVIEW*

Allotting yourself a few minutes to relax in your car or at a nearby coffee shop will give you the chance to settle into a positive mindset before the interview. It is okay to review some of your bullet points and notes you plan to bring in your portfolio to the interview but avoid rehearsing word-for-word responses. Instead, clear your head and be confident that you put in the work and are in a position to ace the interview. Confidence comes from preparation. The better prepared you are for the interview the more genuine your confidence will be.

Some candidates are so excited about a position that they cannot help but feel anxious and desperate to land the job. This mentality will only hurt your prospects. Try not to think of the interview process as pleading with the company for the job. Think of it as a potential partnership - an opportunity for both you and the company. You are going to explain to the company the value you can bring them, and you are also going to find out if the role and compensation are worth your investment in the company. Remember, your skill set is very valuable to the company. If it was not, you would not be there for the interview!

23. TURN OFF YOUR CELL PHONE*

This tip seems obvious and should go without saying but it is worth mentioning that countless interviews have been ruined by vibrating phones. The candidate thought they were in the clear when they turned their ringer off only to discover that the "buzz, buzz, buzz" going off while the interviewer spoke was quite obnoxious and rude. If you want to avoid all risk of your cell phone costing you a job, be extra cautious and turn it completely off before your interview.

24. BE FRIENDLY AND COURTEOUS TO THE RECEPTIONIST*

Remember that the interview technically starts the second you step foot on the company's property. Often, hiring managers gather feedback from the receptionist about their interactions with the candidate when the candidate did not think they needed to be in "interview mode." Many hiring managers admit they have changed their mind about otherwise excellent candidates when finding out they were rude to the receptionist. Receptionists and administrative assistants usually know right away whether the candidate is a good fit with the company's culture.

Be friendly, enthusiastic, and respectful to all company personnel. This includes: security guards, landscapers, executive assistants, interns, and janitors. Smile, introduce yourself, and extend your hand to each person you meet. If you end up waiting in the lobby before your interview, try to spark up some small talk with the receptionist. Instead of sitting in awkward silence, you can use this time to express your interest in the company and turn them into an advocate for your success.

PREPARING FOR INTERVIEW QUESTIONS

25. AVOID MEMORIZING ANSWERS*

Attempting to memorize responses to interview questions will likely lead to a disaster because you can never know with absolute certainty which questions the interviewer will ask. If you spend most of your preparation rehearsing answers to specific questions, you will feel like a deer in the headlights when the interviewer inevitably asks you a question not on your practice list. Further, regurgitated responses will be blatantly obvious to the interviewer. They look for the candidate to use critical thinking skills to articulate a response, not sound like a pre-programmed robot.

When preparing for interview questions, your goal should be to feel comfortable and confident in answering any question that comes up. To achieve a strong level of confidence in answering interview questions, you can follow this simple four-step process during your preparation:

*Be aware of a range of possible questions that could come up during the interview (we will go through a wide range of 100 questions in this book).

*Analyze the questions so you know what the interviewer is looking for in a response (we will analyze each of the 100 questions).

*Instead of developing memorized responses to each question, think about information pertaining to your background, perspective, personality, and experiences. Consider how these perspectives and experiences can be used to answer many different questions.

*Practice answering the questions using these highlighted points. I recommend creating bullet points of information to draw on for the questions (see tip 26).

26. USE BULLET POINTS FOR PRACTICING ANSWERS*

Bullet-pointing notes for interview questions is an excellent way to practice. I recommend creating flash cards with questions on one side and talking points on the other. Once you have your talking points ingrained, you can start practicing the actual responses. You will quickly notice that information from your bullet points can be used to answer many different questions.

As mentioned in tip #25, the goal is to avoid sounding like your answers are scripted. The interview is not an oral test with black and white answers. It needs to be treated like a conversation. Below is an example interview question. First with bullet points and second with an actual word-for-word response.

Question: *Why should we hire you?*

Bullet points:

**Hard-worker, do whatever-it-takes mindset, focus on quality.*

Team player, enjoy group collaboration.

Innovative mindset – think outside the box.

Example Response:

If given the opportunity to join your team, you will immediately notice a few of my characteristics. First, I am a very hard and determined worker. I have always had a "do whatever-it-takes" mindset and I ensure that work with my name on it is rooted in quality. Next, I am a team player who can collaborate within groups to complete a project but am also efficient at working independently when the task calls for it. Finally, I think outside the box to solve problems. I'm not satisfied with simply completing a task the way it has been done in the past; I'm always looking for ways to bring value through innovation.

Now let's consider two scenarios. In scenario 1, you jot down the bullet points above on the back of a notecard. You can probably recall the bullet points in just a couple minutes of practice. In scenario 2, you write out the example response word-for-word and try to memorize it. I don't know about you, but this would take me a lot of time and practice to remember this exact response. Even worse, your expressions would be obvious to the interviewer when trying to recall the memorized answer and you would be highly prone to large pauses or downright panic. If you simply focus on the bullet points, you can practice your response for the question out loud and with family and friends (tips 27 and 28). Your response won't be exactly the same each time but that is a great thing! Even better, you can use your bullet points for more than one question. For example, if the interviewer asks you: *What are some good traits all professionals should possess?* Or *What do you look for in other team members?* Your bullet points can be drawn on for either of these questions. The scripted example answer above could only be used for that exact question which may or may not even be asked. The bullet pointing system allows you to recall a smaller amount of information that can be used for a wider range of questions.

27. PRACTICE ANSWERING QUESTIONS OUT LOUD*

After you have established your bulleted talking points for a wide range of interview questions, practicing responses out loud can be very beneficial in boosting your confidence. As noted in tip 26, do not worry about trying to deliver the exact same response each time. I recommend practicing an answer to a question once or twice before moving on to the next question. You can then come back to that question later and try again. This will prevent you from scripting a word-for-word response to the question. Remember, you want to focus your thoughts on your bulleted talking points. The practice is about being comfortable turning those points into fluid responses.

Most cell phones these days have apps that will enable you to record yourself. I recommend recording your responses and playing them back. Are your responses too fast? Are they too slow? Do the responses flow well? Do you sound confident? A recording device will be beneficial in helping you critique yourself and make any necessary adjustments. When you are comfortable with your responses, I recommend holding mock interviews with friends and family (see tip 28).

28. PRACTICE ANSWERING QUESTIONS WITH FRIENDS AND FAMILY

After practicing your answers out loud, ask a family member or friend to ask you the interview questions. Ideally, it is someone who has experience interviewing in a professional environment or better yet, someone who has conducted interviews. You can provide them with a list of questions and have them select questions at random, so you do not know the order in which they are coming. Ask them to take notes and provide critical feedback on each response. Having them ask you questions in person is ideal but over the phone is beneficial as well.

29. USE THE STAR METHOD FOR BEHAVIORAL QUESTIONS*

Many candidates struggle with behavioral interview questions. They either respond with short oversimplified answers or they drone on with too many details that are not relevant to the question. Interviewers look for candidates to deliver clear and concise answers to behavioral questions. The best way to achieve this is to answer the questions using the STAR method:

Situation:
Explain the background and context of the example you will be discussing. This would possibly include unexpected circumstances or adversity you or your team faced. Be specific with your details to ensure the interviewer understands the context but do not provide unnecessary information that is not relevant to the example.

Task:
Discuss the objective, end goal, or obstacle you needed to overcome. Often the situation and task are discussed together.

Action:
Discuss the planning and execution approach you decided on to achieve the task. Even if it was a team or group situation, remember that the interviewer is focused on your actions. Try to keep the focus of your dialogue on your contributions or leadership when discussing the action.

Result:
Discuss the outcome of the situation. This is the time to discuss the accomplishments that resulted from your actions. Be sure to focus on the positive results and key takeaways from the situation.

In the interview questions and answers section of this book, the STAR method will be used to walk you through example responses to the behavioral questions.

30. QUANTIFY RESPONSES TO BEHAVIORAL QUESTIONS*

Behavioral questions typically start with "Tell me about a time..." or "Give me an example of..." The interviewer is asking the candidate to draw on a prior experience that exemplifies a behavior in a certain situation such as leadership on a project or reaction to adversity. Adding numbers to your answers helps the interviewer better visualize your value. For example:

"After implementing this change, our team decreased customer returns by 30%."

is a much stronger answer than:

"After implementing this change, our team was able to decrease customer returns."

As you practice your interview responses, look for opportunities to add numbers, percentages, and other data that quantify your answers in a positive light. The example responses to behavioral questions in this book will walk you through opportunities to quantify your responses.

31. BE PREPARED TO ACE THE "TELL ME ABOUT YOURSELF" QUESTION*

I emphasize throughout this book that you should be prepared for a wide range of interview questions because you will never know for sure which questions will come your way. However, I can say with almost absolute certainty each interview will start with the "Tell me about yourself" question. It will almost always be the first question of every interview and you can expect it from each person who interviews you. That means if you go through a typical round of interviews with 3 or 4 different interviewers, you can expect to answer it that many times in one day. Since it will usually be the first question of the interview, your answer can build rapport and set the tone for the rest of the discussion.

Many candidates like to use this question to walk the interviewer through their whole resume. However, the interviewer has likely already reviewed your resume. It is okay to highlight some of your background, experience, and current position but avoid going into too many irrelevant details. This is an excellent opportunity to discuss the future. You can use this question to convince the interviewer you are the right person for the job. Your response should be around one minute long and always less than two minutes. The format I typically recommend for answering this question is:

*Your current job (or major and graduation date if you are a student), responsibilities, and experience (number of years on the job).

Example: *"I am an innovative sales director at XYZ Company managing the national product sales division which has seen double digit sales growth in each of the four years under my leadership."*

Or

"I am an honors student and president of the student accounting society within the college of business at XYZ

University expecting to graduate magna cum laude this spring with a major in accounting and minor in finance."

*Your recent experience, promotions, and accolades.

Example: *"Before being promoted to sales director of XYZ Company's national product sales, I was an account executive and regional sales manager for our northeast territory. I won the salesperson of the year award three times within our company while increasing our regional sales revenue by over $2 million. I placed a strong emphasis on implementing and leveraging new CRM technology to bring value to our existing customers while finding opportunities to offer innovative solutions to new customers."*

*Why you want the job and why they should hire you.

Example: *"I really enjoy my current position but in any family owned private business there are limitations on responsibilities and growth. This opportunity excites me because I would be able to bring my skillset and innovative mindset to a company where the sky is the limit."*

This book will analyze this question further and offer another example response in the interview questions and answers section.

32. HAVE A PLAN FOR A "PAUSE" SITUATION*

No matter how prepared you are for the interview, an occasional question can come up that will catch you a bit off guard. It could be an unusual behavioral type scenario you had not given thought to or a question out of left field to test your on-the-spot thinking ability. No matter how odd the question is or how unprepared you feel about answering it, you must remember not to let it hurt your interview. I've seen candidates have excellent interviews up until one of these questions and they panic and let the question blow up the whole interview.

Sometimes we need a little extra time before responding and that is perfectly okay. It's much better to take a few extra seconds than to stumble through a response or, even worse, provide a blatantly obvious made-up answer. Many candidates use "filler" words such as "umm," "so," and "like" in an attempt to think while speaking. They use these words while they try to construct an answer because they are desperately trying to avoid awkward silence. This is a big mistake. The interviewer would rather you pause for a few seconds to consider your response than stumble through it.

It is essential not to panic in these situations. There are a few things you can do to calm your mind down before you take time to formulate a response. Keep in mind that pausing to think is okay, but you typically do not want your pause to occur directly after the question. You want to give the interviewer some type of indication that you are going to take a few seconds to think through your answer. You can repeat part of the question out loud. For example, if the question is "Tell me about a time you failed. What did you learn?" (as a side note, this is not an uncommon question and we will cover it in this book), you can repeat it by saying, "A time I failed…" and then pause for 5-10 seconds to think.

Another way to buy time after the question is to say, "That is a great question…" and then take 5-10 seconds before responding. Remember that anything more than 10 seconds of pausing can turn a normal scenario into uncomfortable silence. Use the brief pause to consider your best response and be confident with it.

33. BRING A CHEAT SHEET WITH YOU*

In the binder or portfolio you bring to the interview, you should include paper with some notes to reference before each interview session begins. I recommend writing down high-level experiences that correlate well with behavioral situations which will be easy to recall. Examples could be:

"Leadership – Took Project Management Role Implementing XYZ Software at XYZ Company."

"Adversity – Team member quit two days before deadline of XYZ project."

"Difficult Boss – Internship at XYZ Company."

These notes are simple and allow you to glance at your notes before each interview session to recall different scenarios. I do not recommend looking down at your cheat sheet when you are asked a question during the interview unless you are completely stumped and you think referencing it quickly will help. Even if you feel like you will not need to reference a cheat sheet, just having it there will increase your confidence and put your mind at ease as you recall past experiences.

I also recommend jotting down your questions for each interviewer. This does not mean you do not need to attempt to remember them on your own, but they will be there just in case you forget. Before each new interview session starts, you can take a quick look at the questions for that respective interviewer.

DURING THE INTERVIEW

34. SHOW HIGH ENERGY AND ENTHUSIASM*

Interviewers look for enthusiasm because it shows them that the candidate is genuinely excited about the opportunity to work for their company. In today's world, many professions have demanding and fast paced environments. The professionals who succeed are those who are highly motivated and enthusiastic about their roles.

Showing enthusiasm does not mean drinking a copious amount of coffee or energy drinks before the interview. This would be a terrible idea. You can show energy and enthusiasm through an upbeat tone in your dialogue and through your mannerisms. With that said, you also want to avoid sounding too over-the-top excited which can come off as fake to the interviewer. The tone of your voice should be similar to the tone you would use when having an interesting discussion with a close friend. You would not speak in a boring monotone voice, but you also would not sound like you are trying to sell a used car either – there is a happy medium between the two. As you practice your responses, record yourself and listen to your tone. You can also ask friends and family to provide feedback as you find the right balance.

35. SHOW CONFIDENCE*

Interviewers seek candidates who can exhibit confidence in a professional manner. The way the candidate handles the pressure of the interview is a sign of how they will react to pressure on the job. Professionals portray confidence by maintaining their composure and facing challenges head-on. It is normal to be a little nervous before an interview. The easiest way to take control of nervousness is to be prepared.

There are a few ways you can portray your confidence before and during the interview. When you first arrive, be sure to extend your hand and provide a firm handshake while smiling and maintaining eye contact. During the interview, make solid eye contact with the interviewer, smile when appropriate, and maintain a smooth and comfortable tone in your voice. People who are nervous tend to speak very fast. Be sure to practice the speed with which you deliver your answers and if you feel yourself speaking too quickly during the interview, slow it down. Another telltale sign of nervousness is fidgeting with your hands or tapping your feet. Focus on remaining still while you are speaking or listening to the interviewer. When the interview concludes, thank the interviewer for the opportunity and offer a firm handshake.

36. DO NOT INTERRUPT THE INTERVIEWER*

In tip #34, we discussed the benefits of showing enthusiasm and energy during the interview. It is common for candidates to connect with something the interviewer is discussing and feel eager about affirming a point or responding to a question before they are finished. The excitement can cause us to interrupt. However, you must avoid this error which can significantly hurt your interview. Be sure to wait until they are completely finished with their question or statement to respond. If you hear something in the middle of their dialogue you would like to respond to, it is okay to write it down and come back to it later on. The interviewer wants to feel in control of the interview, if you interrupt them your chances of getting a job offer will diminish.

37. SHOW INTELLECTUAL CURIOSITY

Companies place a high value on intellectually curious employees because intellectual curiosity is a key contributor to innovation. Employees with this trait are constantly looking for ways to improve existing processes. There are two great opportunities to show intellectual curiosity during the interview. First, when you provide examples to behavioral questions you can focus on times when you challenged an existing process and looked for a better way. You can also show intellectual curiosity through your questions to the interviewer. As discussed in tip #2, you can use your research to ask high level strategic questions that are relevant to the company, industry, or department. Depending on your research, some examples could be:

"What measures does your firm take to ensure client satisfaction is a top priority?"

"How does your department leverage internal controls to mitigate risk?"

"How has your new ERP (enterprise resource planning) system delivered cross functional value?"

38. AVOID CONTROVERSIAL TOPICS*

If your interview is the day before the presidential election and it is all anyone can talk about, you should still avoid it like the plague. There will likely be a period of small talk before the interview questions start to break the ice. This is an opportune time to discuss topics of interest you share with the interviewer (see tip #1) but be sure to avoid controversial topics such as politics and religion. Even if you are confident that the interviewer's beliefs are similar to yours, discussing these topics is a sign of unprofessionalism. If the dialogue moves toward one of these topics (such as an interview question testing your knowledge on a new legislative change), try to remain objective and fact-based instead of interjecting your opinion.

39. TAKE NOTES WHILE THE INTERVIEWER IS SPEAKING*

There will be times when the interviewer discusses names, people, projects, or other specific information about the company that you would like to use for future reference. It is okay to write down some notes while the interviewer speaks. You may even rely on this information at the end of the interview to develop a question. If you bring a portfolio to the interview, you can jot down notes on the paper inside. However, be sure not to write down everything. This can be distracting to the interviewer. Instead, summarize important details while spending the majority of the time maintaining eye contact with the interviewer as they speak.

40. STAY FOCUSED*

Some interviews have four or more sessions and can last many hours. It can get exhausting to speak this long. As the interview goes on, it can be easy to lose focus, but you should keep your mindset on your performance during the interview and the end goal. For a successful interview, you need to be just as clear and focused in your last session as in your first. I do not recommend bringing your own water bottle to the interview. It is very likely that the interviewer will offer you water before it gets started. When you have a break between sessions, be sure to use the restroom and refill your water to ensure you stay hydrated. I also recommend eating a healthy breakfast the morning of the interview to maintain energy (see tip #20).

BODY LANGUAGE

During the interview, communication goes well beyond words. Excellent responses will not make up for the wrong body language which can send bad signals to the interviewer. Below are some body language tips to practice and implement for the interview.

41. SHOW GOOD POSTURE

Reclining too far back in your chair can make you appear disengaged while hunching forward is sloppy and unprofessional. You should sit up with your back straight and maintain good posture throughout the duration of the interview.

42. DO NOT CROSS YOUR ARMS

Crossing your arms can come off as a defensive gesture when you really want to portray comfort and confidence. The best place to rest your arms is on the side rests of the chair.

43. AVOID EXCESSIVE NODDING

Nodding to show agreement or understanding is a great thing. Nodding so much you look like a bobble head is distracting. Use your nods sparingly to show your engagement when the interviewer makes key points.

44. AVOID WANDERING EYES

If your eyes are constantly wandering, it can be a sign of nervousness or, even worse, a sign of being untruthful. I recommend maintaining eye contact while the interviewer is speaking and having eye contact when you finish your own responses. It is okay to break eye contact as you formulate a response as this can be a sign of thinking. While maintaining eye contact, you should avoid a constant deep stare at the interviewer as this can be perceived as aggressive.

45. AVOID FINGER POINTING AND OTHER HAND GESTURES

There is nothing wrong with occasionally using some light hand gestures as you speak but you should avoid anything overly aggressive such as pointing your finger at the interviewer or bumping your fist into your other hand. The safest bet is to practice delivering your responses without using any hand gestures.

46. AVOID FIDGETING

It is common for candidates to fidget during the interview because it is a reaction to being nervous. Be sure to avoid any gestures that make you appear nervous or uncomfortable during the interview.

47. AVOID MISMATCHED EXPRESSIONS

Does your tone sound confident but your facial expressions scream nervousness? This can be a challenge for some candidates. I recommend practicing in front of a mirror and then in front of family and friends to solicit their feedback. Your facial expressions and tone should both be in sync. When the look on your face shows nervousness, your tone will not make up for it. Remember to portray enthusiasm and confidence in both your voice and your body language during the interview.

AFTER THE INTERVIEW

48. SEND THANK YOU EMAILS

I recommend sending separate thank you emails to all the interviewers about 24 hours after the interview. This provides the interviewer with sufficient time to reflect, yet shows your promptness. The email should be brief and to the point. You can thank them for taking the time to interview you and let them know that it was a pleasure to learn more about the company and their career. If they mentioned a topic that you found interesting or took note of, you should consider mentioning it and sending an article link that relates to it. For example, if the interviewer discussed the benefits of implementing a new cloud accounting system, the email could read:

Hi (first name),

Thank you for taking the time to interview me yesterday. It was a pleasure learning more about XYZ Company and your career path. I am excited about the (name of job position) opportunity and feel that it is a strong match for my interests and skillset. I enjoyed hearing about the ways the new cloud accounting system has benefited your department. I found this article on cloud accounting implementations and thought you might find value in reading it: (website link to article)

Sincerely,

(first and last name)
(phone number)

49. SEND THANK YOU LETTERS

You should consider sending out hand-written thank you letters to each interviewer a couple of days after the interview. The letters should be personalized by discussing something the interviewer had discussed with you. It can be a something about their background, the company, or career advice. You can also open the door to further communication by letting them know they can reach out to you at any time while leaving your phone number and email address below your signature.

50. BE PATIENT

The time between the conclusion of the interview and the issuance of the job offer can cause many candidates to lose hope. It is important to accept that the process requires time. Some companies will take a few weeks or even up to a month to inform the candidates of their decision. You should avoid pestering the hiring manager too early on in the process because it can come off as aggressive and work against you. If you have not heard anything back for at least a week after the interview, I recommend sending the hiring manager an email thanking them again for the opportunity to interview and asking when you should expect to know their decision.

PART II:
100 INTERVIEW QUESTIONS, ANALYSIS, AND EXAMPLE RESPONSES

TYPES OF INTERVIEW QUESTIONS

Embracing the correct approach when preparing for interview questions is essential to your success. Before getting into the interview questions, I highly encourage you to read the "Preparing for Interview Questions" tips section if you have not already done so. This section will be beneficial to reference as you read through the questions and start considering your own responses.

Nearly all interview questions fall under one of six categories:

Background and Personality Questions: Questions to learn about the candidate's personality traits, preferences, technical capabilities, and experience.

Behavioral Questions: Questions to assess the candidate's past behavior as a predictor for future behavior. Best answered using the "STAR" method (see tip #29).

Communication Questions: Questions to assess the candidate's soft skills and fit within the company's team dynamics.

Ambition Questions: Questions to assess the candidate's career aspirations and commitment to the company and industry.

Industry and Company Specific Questions: Questions to assess the candidate's interest or knowledge about the organization or a specific profession.

Critical Thinking Questions: Questions to assess the candidate's general intelligence, critical thinking, and decision-making skills.

Each question is identified by its category, but the questions are not grouped. Instead, they are listed in order of their likelihood to come up during a typical interview. You should never be too confident about which questions the interviewer will ask, but some questions are much more common than others. Based on my experience and research, they are ordered from most likely to be asked (#1) to least likely (#99) with question #100 offering more examples of your own questions you can ask at the end of the interview.

1. TELL ME ABOUT YOURSELF.

Question Type:
Background and Personality

Question Analysis:
As mentioned in tip #31, it is safe to assume this question will come up during every interview and it will most likely be the first question. The interviewer is not looking for you to walk them through your whole resume or provide irrelevant details from your past. You should use this question to show your enthusiasm for the opportunity and discuss your skills and experience that make you an excellent fit for the position. I recommend starting with the current, then touching on the past, and finishing with the future. The answer should be roughly one minute in length but never more than two minutes.

What to Avoid:
You should avoid providing too many details that are not

relevant to the interview such as "I grew up in XYZ Town and attended high school at XYZ School. My favorite hobbies are..." Instead, focus on your professional experience (or education if you are still in college) and start with the current, then move to the past, and finish with the future to sell yourself as the right candidate for the position.

Example Response:

I am an ambitious senior supply chain analyst working on the procurement team at XYZ Company. I recently lead a project implementation of new procurement software which resulted in a 30% decrease in our excess and obsolete inventory over the past 6 months. Before joining the procurement team, I was a supply chain analyst on the distribution team where I was responsible for facilitating our product shipments to over 100 wholesalers throughout the country. I enjoy working in my current position, but this opportunity to manage a group while working closely with senior management to implement strategic decisions is exactly what I am looking for in my career.

2. WHAT INTERESTS YOU MOST ABOUT THIS POSITION?

Question Type:

Background and Personality

Question Analysis:

The interviewer will use this question to test whether the candidate has done their homework in assessing the details in the job description. They also want to ensure the candidate's skills and interests align well with the expectations of the position. You should focus your response on discussing how the key elements in the job posting line up well with your skills, interest, and experience.

What to Avoid:

You should avoid discussing items that are not part of the job responsibilities such as the salary or the vacation package. You should also avoid being vague in your response. If you are applying for a sales position, it does not help your cause if your response is simply "meeting with customers." Instead, be more specific by including key elements in the job description.

Example Response:

I understand that this position as a financial analyst requires strong financial planning and forecasting skills. I have experience in a wide range of areas within corporate finance, but I am most interested in financial planning, forecasting, and analysis. Last year, I worked with over five departments to create the operating expense plan for the entire company. I also updated the forecast each quarter and provided variance analysis directly to the controller and CFO. I believe that my interests and expertise in planning and forecasting would be a strong asset to this Company.

3. WHY SHOULD WE HIRE YOU?

Question Type:

Background and Personality

Question Analysis:

Most candidates find this question to be difficult because it puts them on the spot. This is an opportunity to make your personal sales pitch to the interviewer. The interviewer wants to know how you will bring value to the company and what makes you unique from the other candidates. Discussing how your experience and skills are a fit for the job description is key to answering this question. You should be sure to mention at least one trait about yourself that is somewhat unique. Some of the unique traits most employers desire include: innovative, action-oriented, autonomous, detail oriented, analytical, and visionary.

What to Avoid:

You should avoid a response that simply walks through your resume. The interviewer likely already knows your background information. You should also avoid a laundry list of generic traits (hard worker, good communicator, etc.). Instead, focus on the top three reasons why you highly qualified for the position and elaborate on them.

Example Response:

My experience, personality, and desire to succeed make me a perfect fit for this position. Having grown more than 20 sales accounts to over $1,000,000 in annual revenue, I know what it takes to convert Fortune 500 companies into customers. I am a team player who can collaborate to find solutions but also excel *independently when the situation calls for it. Finally, I'm never satisfied with simply completing a task because it has always been done a certain way. I am constantly challenging my work to find opportunities to add value for the company and its customers through innovation.*

4. WHY DID YOU LEAVE (OR WHY ARE YOU LEAVING) YOUR CURRENT POSITION?

Question Type:

Background and Personality

Question Analysis:

This question will come up often when a candidate has recently left or plans to leave their current position to pursue another job. It is important to focus your answer on why the new opportunity interests you and not spend too much time talking about your previous position.

What to Avoid:

Some candidates are tempted to use this question to criticize their former job or employer, but this type of response should be avoided. You should also avoid bringing up anything related to the pay for the new job such as "I'm leaving because this job offers a raise in pay over my current position."

Example Response:

I've enjoyed working at XYZ Company and the experience has helped me grow a lot as a professional. I'm excited about this job because I have the opportunity to take on more responsibility in a leadership role. I also feel that the opportunity allows me to fully utilize my skills and experience.

5. HOW DID YOU FIND OUT ABOUT THIS POSITION?

Question Type:

Background and Personality

Question Analysis:

The interviewer will often use this question to find out which recruiting mechanisms are working well. Some employers offer their employees referral bonuses, so they may also ask the question to confirm that you were referred by a specific employee. You should use this question as an opportunity to show your enthusiasm for the opportunity.

What to Avoid:

You should avoid oversimplified responses such as "I Googled job openings and came across it." If that was the case, you could explain that you were looking online for opportunities related to the position and came across the posting on XYZ Website which seemed like an excellent fit for your skills and interests.

Example Response:

Ryan Wilson who works here in the accounting department saw the job opening and reached out to me because he thought it might be in line with my career aspirations. After reviewing the job description, I was excited about the opportunity because it seemed like an excellent fit for my background and skillset. After speaking to the recruiting manager about the position, I was even more confident that this opportunity is exactly what I am looking for in my career.

6. WHAT IS ONE OF YOUR WEAKNESSES?

Question Type:
Background and Personality

Question Analysis:
This question comes up frequently during most types of interviews. The interviewer is looking for the candidate to provide a candid response to the question. The best way to answer this question is to provide an honest assessment of a real weakness while also discussing how you are actively working to improve in that area.

What to Avoid:
The worst answer you can provide here is "I have no weaknesses." The second worse answer is answering with a positive trait such as "I am a perfectionist." You should also avoid providing a weakness that can be concerning to the interviewer such as "I am always late" or "I often forget to review my work for errors." An ideal answer discusses a common weakness and offers insight into how you are working to improve.

Example Response:

Many people fear public speaking more than death. I think I fall into this category. I do well in situations of one-on-one communication as well as group discussions but when I am up in front of a large audience, I tend to get very nervous which impacts my performance. I recently started working to overcome this fear by giving impromptu presentations to family and friends. I plan on joining the local Toastmasters chapter to practice giving speeches in front of large groups.

7. WHY DID YOU CHANGE CAREER PATHS? (IF APPLICABLE)

Question Type:

Background and Personality

Question Analysis:

The interviewer will almost certainly ask this question if the candidate is applying for a job in a new field. They will use the question to reveal the reasoning behind the career change. They want to be sure that the candidate has done adequate research on the new career path and is committing long-term. You should demonstrate to the interviewer that you have a strong understanding of the job opening as well as your new career path in general. You should focus your response on your enthusiasm for the opportunities in your new career path.

What to Avoid:

You should avoid using this question to criticize a former

employer or boss. The interviewer will have concerns about your commitment to the new career if you come off sounding like you made the change because of a personal conflict. You should also avoid complaining about the type of work you did in your previous career. Instead, focus on the positive aspects of the new career path.

Example Response:

In my previous position in accounting, I worked at a desk the majority of the time, but I would occasionally have the opportunity to meet and interact with our clients. I found that I enjoyed speaking with our clients about solutions for their challenges more than crunching the numbers. I decided to start researching a career in sales and business development and completed three online courses over the past year. My research and training helped me understand the key fundamentals of success in sales and reaffirmed my decision to make a career change. I am excited about this position selling finance software because my previous experience working with companies that are similar in size to your target market will help me identify opportunities to bring them value.

8. WHY HAVE YOU CHANGED JOBS SO FREQUENTLY? (IF APPLICABLE)

Question Type:
Background and Personality

Question Analysis:

A generation ago, employees were much more loyal to their employer. It was common to accept a job as a young adult and remain with the same employer until retirement. In the current economy, employees are more apt to move from company to company when new opportunities come up. It is not uncommon for a resume to show experience with five or more different companies. Unless the candidate's history shows them switching companies every single year, the interviewer is typically not too concerned. They just want to be sure the candidate has good reasoning for their history of job changes. You should be transparent about your employment history but try not to get caught up in any negative details. Focus on positive takeaways from your prior transitions.

What to Avoid:

You should not get defensive about your job history. If you were laid off due to a budget cut or another reason, it is okay to be upfront about it. The interviewer is not looking for excuses, they want you to be genuine in your response. You should also avoid sounding like you will leave a company the second another company offers you a 1% pay increase. If you decided to leave positions in the past for a better opportunity, be sure to explain why the new position was a better fit for your career.

Example Response:

Well, I never expected to work at three different companies over the past five years, but I learned a lot from each experience. I enjoyed working at XYZ Company and had received excellent feedback from my manager but unfortunately the company's sales started to rapidly decline, and they were forced to lay off a large percentage of their IT department. After being laid off, I made the mistake of accepting the first IT job offer I received instead of waiting for a better fit for my career. I ended up leaving XYZ Company 2 to accept my current position which aligns well with my career interests, but I was initially told I would only be required to travel 10% of the time. After a year and a half in my position, the company has required me to travel over 50% of the time which has been difficult on me and my family. I noted that this position requires minimal travel and the work and opportunities company are a strong long-term fit for my career ambitions.

9. MAY WE CONTACT YOUR PREVIOUS (OR CURRENT) EMPLOYER?

Question Type:

Background and Personality

Question Analysis:

This question can be tricky if the candidate is currently employed and does not want their employer to know they are interviewing elsewhere. The interviewer may ask this question with no real intention of contacting your current or past employer. They will often use the question to gauge your reaction to be sure there are no concerning reasons why you would discourage a conversation with your most recent employer.

If you are not currently employed, you should let the interviewer know they can contact your previous employer and provide them with the name of someone who would speak highly of you. If you are currently employed and do not want your employer to know about the interview, you should be upfront in explaining this to the and ask them to reach out to the references on your resume instead.

What to Avoid:

Unless you are trying to keep the interview discreet, you typically do not want to tell the interviewer they cannot contact your former employer. This will usually raise red flags about your work history. If you were let go from your prior job or left under unfavorable circumstances, you should let the interviewer know they can contact your employer but be sure to recommend someone who will speak highly of your work.

Example response for non-discreet interview:
That would be no problem at all. I worked closely on a lot of projects with Stephanie Thompson who is the Marketing Manager at XZY Company. I would be happy to provide you with her contact information.

Example response for a discreet interview:
My current employer does not know that I am interviewing for this position and I would prefer to keep it discreet. However, I do have professional references available I can provide and would encourage you to reach out to them.

10. WHAT IS YOUR GREATEST STRENGTH?

Question Type:
Background and Personality

Question Analysis:
The interviewer will use this question for a couple reasons. They want to find out what you would define as a "great" professional trait. This will tell them a lot about your personality and perspective. They also want to see if your best strength would bring value to the company. Ideally, the strength you discuss is a key trait that is outlined in the job description. After you discuss the strength, you should provide an example that exemplifies it.

What to Avoid:
You should avoid generic answers such as "I am driven" or "I work really hard." Instead, focus on unique strengths that align with the position and would bring tangible value to the company.

Example Response:
I am always thinking about opportunities for innovation. Too often, people become content with a current process and start going through the motions. I never let myself fall into this mindset. At my previous job, I was a sales associate selling satellite internet to those located in rural areas that were stuck with dialup as their only internet option. I felt that too much of our time was wasted calling bad leads. I used Google Maps to identify areas of opportunity and built a database of home

addresses that could likely use our product. I proposed that we send out postcard flyers as a way to increase inbound sales from these areas. After one month, our inbound sales went up by over 20% as a direct result of our new marketing process.

11. WHAT DO YOU KNOW ABOUT THIS COMPANY?

Question Type:
Industry and Company Specific

Question Analysis:
The interviewer will use this question to assess the research done by the candidate prior to the interview. If it is obvious that the candidate did little or no research on the company, it will raise red flags about how they might approach a challenging issue on the job. Tips 4, 5, 6, and 8 discuss excellent methods for researching the company. Great things to speak about here are the company's: core values, mission statement, industry, competition, product offerings, technology, geographic presence and competitive advantages.

What to Avoid:
The interview is not the time to bring up negative press about the company such as "I know they are being sued right now for a product malfunctioning." You should also avoid rehearsing information word-for-word from the company's website such as a paragraph long mission statement. This will not impress the interviewer. It would only show them that you are capable of

memorizing. Instead, bullet point key information when you do your research and discuss it in a conversational tone.

Example Response:

While researching XYZ Company, I noted that your core values include: integrity, reliable, quality, and innovative. I believe strongly in each of these values and strive to make them characteristics of my own work. I know that the company is a market leader and currently holds the most patents in the consumer electronics industry. I also know that they have distribution in over 50 countries throughout the world.

12. TELL ME ABOUT A TIME YOU TOOK A LEADERSHIP ROLE. WHAT WAS THE OUTCOME?

Question Type:
Behavioral

Question Analysis:
Leadership opportunities are not just part of management roles. Companies seek candidates who are strong leaders on projects and in other team settings. They also look for leadership qualities to assess the potential for a transition toward management positions in the future. The interviewer is looking for an example that has a favorable outcome as a direct result of your actions. A leadership example from your prior work experience is ideal but if you cannot come up with a strong

example, an academic project or volunteer opportunity will suffice as well.

What to Avoid:

You should avoid examples that resulted in unfavorable outcomes or were largely uneventful. You should also not include too many unnecessary details. Sticking to the STAR method will help keep the example clear and concise.

Example Response:

S: *In my last position as an account executive, our director of sales unexpectedly left the company three weeks before our annual strategic conference with over 100 of our top clients. Most people in our department started to panic because the director had such an instrumental role in facilitating the lineup of speakers and learning materials, but we did not have time to replace him.*

T: *The vice president of marketing asked me to step up and lead our department in coordinating with the speakers and finalizing all learning materials for the event.*

A: *The first thing I did was schedule a meeting with all five members of our team to map out what was accomplished and what still needed to be done. We created a timeline with the tasks we needed to complete and built in frequent update meetings to ensure we were all on the same page moving forward toward our goal. I also asked each member to come up with three new ideas to improve the learning experience for our clients. We then discussed them as a team and voted on the new ideas that would be incorporated into the event.*

R: *The conference was a success and I even had the opportunity to get up on stage and give a short presentation on one of the new ideas our team developed. Our clients had nothing but positive feedback about their experience and our vice president was very appreciative of my leadership.*

13. WHAT ARE THREE CHARACTERISTICS YOUR CO-WORKERS WOULD USE TO DESCRIBE YOU?

Question Type:
Background and Personality

Question Analysis:
The interviewer will use this question to gauge whether the candidate's characteristics are a strong fit for the position. They also want to know if the candidate would fit in well with the company dynamics. An excellent way to come up with positive characteristics your co-workers would use to describe you is to think back to any positive feedback they provided while working closely together. Ideally, the characteristics you use in your response will align well with those sought after in the job description.

What to Avoid:
You should avoid generic responses such as "hard working" or "positive." You should also avoid traits that are not professional or specific to the job such as "outgoing" or "friendly."

Example Response:

My co-workers would describe me as dependable, organized, and innovative. When there is a tight deadline tied to my work, they know they can rely on me to complete it on time and have it done correct the first time. They would also point out that I frequently propose opportunities for improving existing processes and implementing new value-added measures.

14. ARE YOU INTERVIEWING AT OTHER COMPANIES?

Question Type:

Ambition

Question Analysis:

The interviewer may ask this question for a number of reasons. Often, they want to know where a candidate is in the search process and whether the candidate is entertaining other offers. This knowledge may influence the timing of their offer as well as the terms of the compensation package. They might also use the question to validate the strength of the candidate by assessing their popularity with other potential employers. If you have already interviewed with competitors or have interviews coming up, it can be to your advantage to mention so but you should emphasize your interest and excitement in the current opportunity.

What to Avoid:

Assuming you are conducting a traditional search for a new job, you should typically avoid telling the interviewer you are not interviewing elsewhere. It can make you appear desperate for the position and the interviewer might wonder why you have not received other interviews. If you have applied at other companies but do not have any other outside interviews at the time, you can mention that you are in different phases of exploring opportunities with a few other companies. Perhaps you are not actively seeking other opportunities and the interviewer's company specifically sought you out for the job or you are pursuing this particular role for its unique fit for your career goals. In this case, speak succinctly about your reasoning for taking the interview. It goes without saying, but you should never lie to the interviewer. It is okay to be vague, but do not say you have other interviews if that is not true.

15. WHERE DO YOU SEE YOURSELF IN FIVE YEARS?

Question Type:
Ambition

Question Analysis:
This question will help the interviewer gauge how committed the candidate is to the company. The question can catch some candidates off guard because they are so focused in on the position but have not given much thought to the future. The answer should be dependent on the position and industry. Some industries offer a lot of opportunities and growth without a definitive path to management. Other industries, such as public accounting, have a clear five or six-year path to a management position. It is important to conduct research on

the position and emphasize your desire to embrace opportunities to grow within the company.

What to Avoid:

You should avoid responses that indicate complacency such as "I'll be happy if I am in this position five years from now." Interviewers typically look for candidates to express an eagerness to grow and advance within the company. You should also avoid unrealistic and smug responses such as "CEO of the company" or "I plan to have your job."

Example Response:

One of the main reasons I applied for this position was for the chance to work at a company that offers so many growth opportunities to its employees. Over the next five years I see myself taking advantage of those opportunities by taking on additional responsibilities as an individual contributor and as part of a team. As I establish credibility and continue to grow over the next five years, I see myself moving into a management or leadership position within the finance department.

16. WHY DO YOU WANT TO WORK HERE?

Question Type:

Ambition

Question Analysis:

The interviewer will use this question to ensure the candidate is interested in the position for the right reasons and has done some homework on the company. Your answer should include specifics about the company that show a strong level of interest and enthusiasm.

What to Avoid:

You should avoid responses that are overly generic such as "I want to work here because this is an excellent company." The interviewer will view this response as an indication that did not do sufficient research on the position or company. You should also avoid misinformed responses. Be sure to have your facts straight about the company and position and avoid bringing up items you are not sure about.

Example Response:

I first became interested in XYZ Company when I saw Forbes Magazine list it as a top 100 company to work for in the world. I did further research and found that it is known for fostering a collaborative and innovative culture. This type of work setting is exactly what I am looking for and I feel that my personality and aspirations would be a perfect fit. I am also very excited about the potential opportunity to work on the supply chain team to leverage my prior experience with SAP while supporting procurement teams all over the world.

17. WHY DID YOU CHOOSE TO GO INTO THIS PROFESSION?

Question Type:
Ambition

Question Analysis:

The interviewer will use this question to find out if the candidate researched the profession and orchestrated a calculated plan or if it was more random chance that led them into the profession. Even if there were random variables that lead you down your career path, your answer should focus on the purposeful decisions you made to move forward in your profession as well as the experience that affirmed that decision. It will tell the interviewer you understand the industry and have a vested interest in sticking around long-term. It will also show that you are methodical when making significant decisions.

What to Avoid:

You should avoid placing too much emphasis on random events that factored into your career path. If there were unexpected events that lead you down your path, you can touch on them but emphasize how your research or experience affirmed your decision.

Example Response:

I had always wanted to pursue a career in technology and wanted to ensure that I went into a field that had diverse opportunities and was on the cutting edge of innovation. After speaking with a few professors and career advisors my freshman year of college, I was confident that I wanted to become a web developer. I then made it my mission to connect with web developers in the area to get a better sense of their day-to-day work. That opened the door for an internship and eventual first job after college. My experience as a web developer has affirmed my decision to go into the profession. Looking back on my decision, I would not change a thing.

18. DESCRIBE YOUR IDEAL BOSS.

Question Type:
Background and Personality

Question Analysis:
Interviewers will usually ask this question to get a sense of the type of leadership style the candidate works best under. The answer will provide them with a better understanding of the candidate's work style. In your response, you should demonstrate that you have no problem working independently but also have an appreciation and respect for authority. You should try to focus your answer in on characteristics that are conducive to the company's values and culture.

What to Avoid:
Some interviewers use this question as a test to see whether the candidate will criticize a former boss. You should avoid responses that imply you had a negative relationship with a prior boss. The interviewer may take the criticism of a former boss as a sign that you are difficult to manage.

Example Response:
I've been fortunate to work for a couple excellent bosses in the past. To me, an ideal boss leads by example and helps to create shared vision for the team. Their own actions have a large impact on team morale and can be an inspiration to those

around them. An ideal boss trusts their employees to get the job done but possesses excellent communication skills when their input is needed. Finally, an ideal boss maintains a positive outlook and focuses on solutions instead of looking for blame when something goes wrong.

19. TELL ME ABOUT A TIME YOU FAILED. WHAT DID YOU LEARN?

Question Type:

Behavioral

Question Analysis:

Since the purpose of the interview is to leave a highly positive impression, talking about failure can be difficult for most candidates. The interviewer will ask this question because they want to know that the candidate can acknowledge and learn from failure. Failure can be ambiguous, so it can be beneficial to define what failure means to you before providing an example. In your example, you should discuss why you failed and how you learned from it.

What to Avoid:

You should avoid an underwhelming example such as "I was only rated a four out of five on my employee evaluation." The interviewer knows that everyone fails occasionally so you should discuss a genuine example. With that said, you should not discuss any examples that would scare the interviewer such as "I fell for a financial phishing scam and cost our company a million dollars." You should avoid discussing a substantial lapse in judgement or a sloppy error.

Example Response:

S: *Most people only think of failure as events with significant consequences, but I consider myself to have failed each time I do not meet my goals and expectations. The key for me is to recognize even the smallest of failures so that I can learn from them and make adjustments. In my current role as a cost accountant, I am in charge of producing our annual budget for our largest production plant.*

T: *My first year creating the budget, I met with the managers at the plant to discuss the material, labor, and overhead projections for the upcoming fiscal year. The production plan seemed straight forward for the year, which lead to my confidence in compiling the budget. However, the managers forgot to mention a pending capital expenditure project and I failed to review the project management system to identify it.*

A: *The project ended up going through in the current year and as a result, the actual depreciation expense for the year was 20% higher than in my budget. In my explanation of the variance, I was honest about the fact that I neglected to reference the project management system to substantiate the budget inputs for new projects.*

R: *I quickly learned that when creating forecasts and budgets, validating information and data is just as important as collecting it. Going forward, I developed a systematic approach to substantiate all information and assumptions in my budgets.*

In each of the prior three years, my budget to actual variances have been the lowest in our whole department.

20. WHAT IS A SIGNIFICANT CHALLENGE FACING THE PROFESSION (ACCOUNTING, FINANCE, NURSING, ENGINEERING, ETC.) TODAY?

Question Type:
Industry and Company Specific

Question Analysis:
The interviewer will use this question to assess the candidate's awareness of the current hot topics in the profession. They want to see that the candidate has not only followed news and trends in the profession but also considered the ramifications of some of the challenges it faces. Your answer should demonstrate that you have an inherent interest in the profession and have thought through how recent events or trends could disrupt it.

What to Avoid:
You should try to avoid answers that do not discuss why the challenges are specific to the profession such as "outsourcing is eliminating jobs." Your answer should explain the issue and then discuss why it is particularly challenging to your profession.

Example response (accounting profession):
Cloud accounting programs and applications have had a significant impact on the profession. My opinion is that they can be both a challenge and an opportunity. The cloud

technology today has made it much easier for those who do not necessarily have accounting or bookkeeping experience to book entries and access financial reporting. The opportunity is that the technology has enabled accountants and financial analysts to focus less on the data entry and more on the reporting and decision making. The challenge is that many businesses are relying too heavily on software and technology and not utilizing the skills of a qualified accountant. This can save them resources in the short-term but can also increase the risk of costly reporting or regulatory errors.

21. TELL ME ABOUT A TIME WHEN YOU WENT ABOVE AND BEYOND EXPECTATIONS FOR A PROJECT OR ASSIGNMENT.

Question Type:
Behavioral

Question Analysis:
One of the most common performance ratings for a hardworking and competent employee is "meets expectations" however, there will be opportunities when an employee should think outside of the box and go above and beyond the call of duty. Interviewers want to know that the candidate is willing to embrace these opportunities instead of shying away from them. You should discuss an example of a time when you identified an

opportunity to exceed expectations and took advantage of it to bring value to your team or to a customer.

What to Avoid:

You should avoid opportunistic dialogue such as "I always exceed expectations." The interviewer will know this is not a realistic response. You should avoid examples that would be expected of any normal hard-working employee such as "I had a tight deadline coming up, so I worked 50 hours one week instead of my normal 40."

Example Response:

S/T: *In my previous position as a web developer, I was assigned to a project to help a new customer integrate a payment processor for their ecommerce platform. As I was reviewing their website code, I noticed some unrelated HTML errors that were hurting their search engine optimization. I estimated that it would take me an extra twelve hours to fix the code, but I had no extra time in my schedule.*

A: *I explained the situation to my manager and asked for permission to do the work for the customer outside of my current work commitments. She was impressed that I took the initiative to bring additional value to a new customer at the expense of my evenings over the next week. I informed the customer about the errors and explained the SEO value it would bring if I corrected them.*

R: *Both my manager and our customer were appreciative that I was willing to work the extra hours at no additional charge to correct the issue for them. They ended up choosing our firm for a major project three months later and mentioned their earlier experience working with me as a deciding factor.*

22. TELL ME ABOUT A TIME YOU HAD TO MEET A TIGHT DEADLINE. WHAT WAS THE OUTCOME?

Question Type:

Behavioral

Question Analysis:

The interviewer will ask this question to assess how well the candidate works under pressure and to see if they are willing to go the extra mile. You should provide an example of an unexpected situation that involved careful planning and required you to go above and beyond normal expectations.

What to Avoid:

You should avoid providing an example that is associated with a routine task such as "our monthly report was due the next day, but I had not started it yet" because you likely would have known about the deadline in advance, so it can appear as though it is only a tight deadline due to poor planning. Unless there was a significant unforeseen circumstance, you should also avoid discussing an example of a tight deadline which you or your team were not able to meet it.

Example Response:

S: *In my previous role as a systems analyst, I lead a project to implement an EDI integration for a client's new procurement software.*

T: *Two weeks before the project deadline, the client informed us of a significant issue with their legacy software which was having a major impact on their day-to-day business. They asked if we could accelerate our timeline to deliver our project in five days. My manager and I discussed the situation and agreed to let the client know we would do everything we could to meet their new request.*

A: *I brought our team together to explain the situation and let them know that we would be focusing our time exclusively on this project to try to meet the accelerated deadline. I mapped out all remaining tasks on a whiteboard and we agreed on completion dates for each task over the next five days. I also scheduled daily update meetings to ensure we were staying on track and available to each other when issues came up.*

T: *We worked 14 hours per day over the next five days but through our collaboration and perseverance we completed the project on time. The client was extremely happy with results of the project and our manager gave each of us three extra vacation days for our hard work.*

23. TELL ME ABOUT A TIME YOU DISAGREED WITH YOUR BOSS. HOW DID YOU HANDLE IT?

Question Type:

Behavioral

Question Analysis:

The interviewer will use this question to assess how well the candidate handles a disagreement with someone in an authoritative position. The response will say a lot about the type of working relationship the candidate might have with a future boss. Your example should show that you have confidence in speaking candidly with your boss while still respecting their point of view and authority. You should try to think of a situation in which you disagreed with a decision or direction of a project, but offered an alternative solution.

What to Avoid:

In your example, you should avoid personally criticizing your boss. This can raise a warning flag about your character. You should also avoid examples in which you raised the disagreement with your boss in the presence of other team members. Unless your boss encouraged feedback in a group setting, disagreements with those in authority should be handled in a one-on-one setting.

Example Response:

S: *In a prior role as a procurement analyst, I was on a team that worked on procurement process efficiency through the measurement of purchasing history and inventory turnover trends. In an effort to add more reporting functionality to our purchasing history, our boss worked on a project to switch us over to a new software package.*

T: *Although the reporting functionality had improved, the new software did not integrate directly with our company's ERP system, so we were required to manually upload our purchase history which often took us hours to do.*

A: *I set up a meeting with my boss to explain my experience and concerns with the software. I first told him that I appreciated his hard work in seeking to find better reporting solutions. I then explained that I felt the benefits of the new software were outweighed by the time it took our team to manually add the purchasing history data which slowed down our analysis. As an alternative solution, I showed him documentation of research I had done on comparable software that could be integrated with our ERP system.*

R: *My boss was appreciative of me being upfront and honest about the change. He also thanked me for my research on the software solution I came up with and one month later we ended up switching over to it.*

24. WHAT DO YOU LIKE MOST ABOUT WORKING IN THIS INDUSTRY?

Question Type:

Industry and Company Specific

Question Analysis:

The interviewer will ask this question for a couple reasons. First, a new hire is an investment for the company, so they want to validate the candidate's passion and long-term commitment to the industry. They will also use the question to see how well the response aligns with the duties of the job. When discussing your favorite aspects about the industry, be sure to highlight those that are highly relevant to the position.

What to Avoid:

You should avoid discussing characteristics that do not pertain to the position. For example, if you are interviewing for a marketing position and the job description desires competency in Adobe Photoshop, you would not want to express how much you love working with Affinity Photo (Mac competitor to Photoshop). You should also try not to be too vague in your response. "I love that I get to work with people" does not sound nearly as good as "I enjoy working directly with clients to diagnose their challenges and offer solutions that bring them a better return on investment on their advertising budgets."

Example Response:

The thing I enjoy most about offering software solutions in the sales industry is that no two days are ever the same. I have the opportunity to work with such a wide range of clients who possess diverse challenges and needs for their human resource systems. I take pleasure in fostering client relationships. To me, success looks like a client reaching out for help with confidence that I can solve their problem. Believe it or not, I also really enjoy the travel associated with this industry. I consider it an opportunity to be able to explore new cities while I am traveling to meet with current and prospective clients.

25. WHAT WAS THE MOST DIFFICULT DECISION YOU HAVE MADE IN THE PAST YEAR?

Question Type:

Behavioral

Question Analysis:

Candidates without management experience will often get tripped up over this question because they have not had to make what would traditionally be considered a difficult decision such as cutting a budget or laying off an employee. However, there are plenty of opportunities to discuss difficult decisions outside of management roles. The interviewer is looking for an answer that demonstrates rationale and strong problem-solving skills. You should discuss an example that shows your ability to weigh options and critically think through the situation before coming to the decision. Some examples of tough decisions include: reporting unethical behavior, providing a negative review for a co-worker, choosing a new vendor, and turning down a promotion.

What to Avoid:

You should avoid discussing personal decisions that are not relevant to the position such as "I decided to purchase my first home last year" or "three months ago, I decided it was time to break it off with my fiancé." The interviewer is looking for your decision-making capabilities in a professional setting. Your answer should include the result of your decision, so you should avoid examples where the decision lead to an unfavorable outcome.

Example Response:

S/T: *In a previous role selling professional services for IT projects, I was offered a promotion to be our company's Midwest resource services manager. I was honored to be offered the promotion and asked my boss for a few days to consider it. The new position would have increased my responsibilities while offering a raise in pay. At the time, I was in critical stages of a few projects with my clients. I was also making inroads with prospective clients that would soon lead to new business. Before the promotion came up, I had a strong interest in exploring future opportunities within the company's marketing team which would be a change to a new department.*

A: *I set up a meeting with my boss to discuss my desire to remain in my current position as well as my inclination to find an opportunity in the marketing department for my next career move.*

R: *At first, he was a little surprised that I decided to turn down the promotion, but he agreed with me that I brought the most value to our clients by remaining in my current position. He thanked me for my honest assessment and connected me with a manager in the marketing department to discuss future opportunities.*

26. WHAT MOTIVATES YOU?

Question Type:
Ambition

Question Analysis:
Candidates often struggle with this question because it is so broad in nature. The interviewer is typically using the question to understand what type of work is encouraging and fulfilling to the candidate. Coming up with an answer does require some personal reflection but ultimately your response should be centered around positive results or characteristics in the professional setting. Ideally, your motivation comes from something that aligns well with the company's culture.

What to Avoid:
Some candidates see this as such a broad question that they answer it with personal examples such as "my husband and kids" or "my lake cottage" but the interviewer is typically looking for motivation from a professional perspective.

Example Response:
I am motivated by a team culture that encourages collaboration and innovation. When team members are encouraged to work together to change things for the better, it brings lasting value to the whole organization. There is nothing I like more than envisioning a better way to do something and seeing it come to life.

27. WHAT DO YOU LIKE TO DO OUTSIDE OF WORK?

Question Type:
Background and Personality

Question Analysis:
This may seem like a "softball" question but the interviewer will be paying close attention to your response to see if you are a good fit for the company's culture. Employers look for candidates who make the most of their free time. Your answer should be focused on activities that benefit your own wellbeing and the wellbeing of others in the community.

What to Avoid:
You should avoid discussing activities that sound unprofessional such as "I enjoy drinking and tailgating every Saturday during football season" or "I play video games each night." You should also be careful not to provide a dry response that makes it sound like you have no hobbies. This can create a negative perception about your personality in the eyes of the interviewer.

Example Response:
I am an avid golfer and fly fisherman. I try to play at least one round of golf each week during the spring and summer and I just got back from a fly fishing trip in Yellowstone National Park. I also enjoy giving back to the local community. I volunteer two days a month at the local VA hospital and am on the Board of our local Habitat for Humanity chapter.

28. WHAT IS YOUR MANAGEMENT STYLE?

Question Type:

Background and Personality

Question Analysis:

This question is very common when interviewing for management or supervisor positions but may also come up for any role that requires some level of leadership capability. The interviewer wants to know if your management style would be effective for the position and align well with the company's leadership culture. You should focus your response on your leadership traits that would fit well within the company and bring value to the position.

What to Avoid:

You should avoid using absolute words to describe your management style such as "always," "never," or "must." For example, scheduling regular team meetings to encourage team discussion and collaboration is an excellent tactic but if you say, "whenever an issue arises, I always schedule a group meeting to collaborate until we find an answer," it sounds like you react the same way to every problem. You should discuss your style with an emphasis on being able to adapt to a specific situation or to the unique personality traits of your team members.

Example Response:

I believe that the most effective managers are capable of adapting their style to the unique traits of each team member to empower them to reach their full potential. My typical management style is to lead by example, use clear and concise communication, encourage collaboration, and provide constructive feedback. As I get to know my team members, I will often make adjustments to my style to help bring more value to the team. For example, I typically like to meet with each of my team members once per month to discuss their concerns and offer constructive feedback. Last year, I noticed that one of my new team members was second guessing her work which was causing her to fall behind on a project. I decided to adjust my meeting schedule with her to once per week, so I could offer her more regular feedback. I immediately started to see an increase in her confidence which lead to better efficiency in her work. Eventually, she felt comfortable enough to reduce our meeting schedule to once per month. She mentioned that the weekly feedback I offered was a key element in helping her build up her confidence on our team.

29. WHY SHOULD WE HIRE YOU OVER THE OTHER CANDIDATES?

Question Type:

Background and Personality

Question Analysis:

This question is almost identical to question #3 but when some candidates are asked to compare themselves to the other candidates, they feel a sense of pressure to oversell themselves to the point of sounding like a used car salesman. However, it is important to remember that you will typically not earn the job offer on a single "grand slam" response. It is earned over the course of a full interview. The interviewer will use this question to learn more about the candidate's strengths and any type of unique value they would bring to the position. You should focus your answer on your strengths that correspond well with the job requirements and try to discuss at least one unique trait that would be attractive to the company.

What to Avoid:

Even though the question invites you to do so, you should avoid making any assumptions about the other candidates such as "I would work harder than any of the other candidates." Negative statements about candidates you likely do not even know can come off as presumptuous and arrogant. Instead, you can acknowledge that you cannot speak for the other candidates, but you feel confident that you are the right fit for the position.

Example Response:

Well, I cannot speak with regard to the other candidates, but I can tell you why I am an excellent fit for the position. My experience leading the development of over 25 successful web applications has put me in a position to understand what it takes to strategize, plan, and execute any type of coding project. My experience leading teams has taught me strong organizational and motivational skills. Aside from my strong skillset that aligns with the position, I am always looking to bring added value to any process or project through innovation. I am never content with a system or process if there is a more effective or efficient way. I typically drive innovation by collaborating with both internal and external resources and by leveraging new technology.

30. TELL ME ABOUT A TIME YOU SET A CHALLENGING GOAL FOR YOURSELF. HOW DID YOU ENSURE THAT YOU ACHIEVED IT?

Question Type:

Behavioral

Question Analysis:

The interviewer will use this question to get a better sense of the candidate's ambition and initiative. They also want to know the strength of the candidate's planning skills when faced with a difficult challenge. In your response, you should focus the discussion around the planning and analysis that enabled you to take calculated actions to achieve your goal.

What to Avoid:

If you have professional experience on your resume, you should typically avoid discussing personal goals such as "I set a goal to lose 50 pounds" or "my goal was to complete a marathon." Instead try to draw on a goal you achieved that relates to your profession. You should also avoid trivial goals such as "I set a goal to arrive at work by 8:30 AM each day."

Example Response:

S: *In my previous role as an IT security analyst, I noted that all managers and directors in my department had the Certified Information Systems Security Professional (CISSP) certification in their email signature. I spoke with my manager and learned that the company highly encouraged the certification for IT employees who sought promotions and leadership opportunities.*

T: *I wanted to place myself in a position to be considered for growth opportunities in our department, so I set a personal goal to pass the CISSP exam within three months. The exam is six hours long and covers eight different subjects, so I knew I would need to create and execute a detailed plan to achieve my goal.*

A: *Before I started studying for the exam, I reviewed the study materials and spoke with co-workers who had passed the exam to determine the expected number of study hours. I looked through my calendar for the next three months to identify study time outside of the working days and on weekends. After determining that I would need roughly 100 hours to study for the exam, I created a robust plan assigning sections of the preparation materials to each study session on my calendar.*

R: *It was a strenuous three months, but I remained focused on my end goal to ensure I stayed on task with my study plan. I ended up acing the exam and I accepted a promotion within our department later that year.*

31. WHAT WOULD YOUR BOSS SAY IS AN AREA YOU COULD IMPROVE ON?

Question Type:
Background and Personality

Question Analysis:
The interviewer will use this question to assess how well the candidate embraces critical feedback. No matter how strong a performance review might be, most managers will offer up at least one area for improvement. The interviewer is looking for the candidate to be candid about an area for improvement and discuss how they are taking action. Ideally, your response would discuss an area you are new to and investing time to improve.

What to Avoid:
You should avoid criticizing your boss's judgement. A response such as "my boss told me I need to pay better attention to detail but I disagree with her assessment" will not go over well with the interviewer. It will portray you as someone who is not receptive to critical feedback from superiors. You should also avoid saying something such as "my boss has never suggested an area for improvement." Remember that this question is a hypothetical. If your boss has not provided critical feedback, then you can still come up with your own area for self-improvement. Finally, you should avoid discussing areas that would be concerning to the interviewer. If you are interviewing for a sales position and you mention that you need to become better at communicating with customers, you will create a cause for concern.

Example Response:

My boss would say I could get better at recognizing when my work load is at full capacity and delegating work. I recently moved into a supervisor role, but I still put too much on my own plate which causes me unnecessary stress. When tasks and projects come up I tend to gravitate toward taking full ownership over them instead of working with my team to find out who is in the best position to do the work.

I recently implemented weekly update meetings with my team so that we can run through everyone's workload and availability. These meetings have helped me identify opportunities to delegate project work throughout our team to create a better balance for everyone.

32. WHY IS THERE A GAP IN YOUR EMPLOYMENT HISTORY? (IF APPLICABLE)

Question Type:

Background and Personality

Question Analysis:

If the interviewer asks this question they are looking for an upfront and honest response. The best way to approach this question largely depends on the reason for the gap. If you were laid off, you should provide some details of the situation and discuss why the company decided to reduce headcount. If you took a leave of absence, you can explain the situation from a high level but there is no need to go into too many personal details. For example, "I had a health scare I needed to resolve" or "a family member became ill and needed my full attention" is enough detail. You should try to incorporate positive items in your employment history before and after the gap. It is also beneficial if you can discuss your ambitious intentions during the gap period.

What to Avoid:

You should avoid getting defensive with your response. Your answer should not be centered around any excuses with past employment. Whether it was a result of a prior job or a personal reason that resulted in the gap, you should avoid going into too many unnecessary details.

Example Response:

When I previously worked at XYZ Company, they unexpectedly lost their largest customer and needed to take drastic action to stay in business. 25% of the sales force was laid off including most members on my team. It felt like a punch in the gut, but I understood the Company did not have much of a choice.

As I considered my next steps, I decided that it was important not to jump at the first opportunity but instead take the time to find the right fit for my career. I treated the job search like a full-time position, spending most of my days making new connections and setting up coffee or lunch meetings with business contacts in the area. I also made time to take a two-week online sales training course I had been interested in for over a year. After 4 months of networking and consideration, I decided to accept a position for a territory sales manager at XYZ Company.

33. WHAT ARE THREE SKILLS ALL PROFESSIONALS IN THIS FIELD SHOULD POSSESS?

Question Type:

Industry and Company Specific

Question Analysis:

The interviewer will likely ask this question using the name of the profession such as "What are three skills all accountants should possess?" You should be prepared to discuss skills that are highly relevant to your profession and align closely with the job description. The interviewer is typically looking for the candidate to hone in on certain skill sets that are a must for the profession (i.e. excellent verbal communication skills for a nurse). The following skills are highly relevant to nearly all professions: Effective communicator, attention to detail, excellent planner, and strong time management.

What to Avoid:

Your answer should avoid overly generic skills that are presumed for all professionals such as "hard worker." Your answer should also not be a laundry list of skills. Be sure to discuss how each skill benefits the professional in their respective field.

Example Response:

(Example response is for accountants)

Successful accountants focus on attention to detail to ensure their work is complete and accurate. We work in a profession where small mistakes can have profound consequences. Attention to detail in this profession means fully understanding the scope of the work and expectations before completing it. It also means critical self-reviews before finalizing our work.

Accountants should also be excellent at planning their work at a micro and macro level. Time management is essential to staying on track and meeting deadlines.

Finally, all successful accountants should be effective communicators. Whether it is meeting with a boss, collaborating with team members, or discussing an issue with a client, accountants need to have strong written and verbal communication skills.

34. WHAT WAS SOMETHING YOU DID NOT LIKE ABOUT YOUR PREVIOUS (OR CURRENT) POSITION?

Question Type:

Background and Personality

Question Analysis:

This can be a tricky question because candidates are often tempted to heavily criticize their previous job or employer, but this can reflect poorly on the candidate's own personality and professionalism. You should discuss why you did not prefer a certain management style, a team dynamic, or a job limitation from a professional perspective.

What to Avoid:

Unless something drastic happened (such as fraud or harassment), it is important to stay away from character attacks or interoffice drama because the interviewer may associate it with your own personality. It is also wise to avoid criticism of common challenges that occur in most work environments such as "too much stress," "long hours," or "a demanding boss." These answers may lead to the interviewer questioning whether the candidate can handle adversity which will come up often in most positions.

Example Response:

Overall, I was really satisfied with my previous position. I worked with a great team and grew as a professional. I do wish I would have had more leadership opportunities in my previous role. The company was traditional in the sense that most project work was initiated and micro managed by the company's leadership. I thrive in an environment that offers leadership opportunities for all employees.

35. TELL ME ABOUT A TIME YOU HAD TO WORK CLOSELY WITH SOMEONE WHOSE PERSONALITY WAS MUCH DIFFERENT THAN YOURS. WHAT WAS THE OUTCOME?

Question Type:

Behavioral

Question Analysis:

The interviewer will use this question to assess the candidate's team working capabilities. They want to know that the candidate possesses sufficient emotional intelligence to successfully adapt to the various personalities of co-workers. You should discuss an example that shows your ability to effectively communicate with a differing personality to achieve the desired results.

What to Avoid:

You should avoid criticizing a team member's personality. You should also avoid examples of working around another team member or excluding them from the work. The interviewer wants to see that you are able to adapt to various situations to find positive ways to work together with other team members.

Example Response:

S/T: *Last year I lead a system implementation project with four other team members. I scheduled weekly update meetings to discuss the status of the project and to encourage collaboration on technical issues we were encountering. I noticed that one of our team members was extremely quiet during our team meetings, but he would often email me afterwards with excellent insight and ideas about the issues we had just discussed in the team setting. Not hearing his ideas until after our meetings was hurting our team collaboration. It was also inefficient for me to communicate his ideas back to the team versus all of us discussing them during the meetings.*

A: I looked into his experience and employment history and noted that he had just graduated from college and joined the company one month prior. Instead of talking with him about the issue during the next team meeting, I decided to schedule a one-on-one meeting. I explained to him that I was a bit nervous and shy when I first started with the company and that it was completely normal. I also tried to boost his confidence by explaining how valuable his follow up ideas had been toward the project. I explained the benefits of speaking up during team meetings but made sure not to make him feel too much pressure.

R: Over the course of the next few weeks we all started to observe him grow more comfortable with sharing his input during the team meetings. While he may be disposed to a more reserved personality, the ability to acknowledge that and work with him enabled us to use his talents to add more value to our team.

36. DO YOU PREFER WORKING IN A TEAM SETTING OR INDEPENDENTLY?

Question Type:
Background and Personality

Question Analysis:
This question can be tricky to some candidates because it sounds as if the interviewer is asking them to take up a definitive preference for one setting over the other. However, most positions require candidates to work both independently and within a group. Unless the job description explicitly calls for working independently or in a team setting at all times, the best response is to explain that you are comfortable working in both environments.

What to Avoid:
It is okay if you prefer working independently over working with a team or vice versa but you should avoid making a bold preference in your answer. The interviewer may view your strong preference as a sign that you are weak in the other area.

Example Response:
It largely depends on the situation. Some projects and tasks are best accomplished through team work and collaboration while others are more effectively completed through independent work. I have a do-whatever-it-takes mindset and feel comfortable as a team player collaborating in a group setting but can also buckle down and work independently when needed.

37. DID YOU GET ALONG WITH YOUR PRIOR BOSS?

Question Type:

Background and Personality

Question Analysis:

The interviewer will use this question to get a better sense of the candidate's ability to work well with superiors. The interviewer wants to know whether you create or burn bridges. You will usually only hurt yourself by heavily criticizing your previous or current boss. Unless your boss did something highly unethical or illegal, you should focus on a positive answer.

What to Avoid:

You should avoid personal insults and character attacks when describing your previous boss. If your answer is strongly critical of your boss, the interviewer will likely view you as someone who does not respect superiors or get along well with co-workers.

Example Response:

I enjoyed working for my former boss. She never let her team get bored with their work. I was always presented with new challenges and learning opportunities. She also placed a strong emphasis on team communication and had an open-door policy for new ideas. Her management style helped me grow as a professional.

38. WHAT TYPE OF SALARY ARE YOU SEEKING?

Question Type:
Background and Personality

Question Analysis:
You should avoid a specific dollar amount for this question. Instead, focus your answer on your enthusiasm for the position and desire to receive a competitive offer. Effective salary negotiators typically avoid being the first one to throw out a figure.

What to Avoid:
You should avoid discussing a specific desired salary figure in your response.

Example Response:
I am excited about the opportunities that come with this position but have not focused on a specific salary figure. If you were to offer me the job, I would hope to get an offer that is competitive with the salary range for this position while taking into consideration my experience and skillset.

39. TELL ME ABOUT A TIME YOU HAD TO DEAL WITH A DIFFICULT CO-WORKER. WHAT WAS THE OUTCOME?

Question Type:
Behavioral

Question Analysis:

The interviewer will ask this question to assess the candidate's ability to manage conflict in the work setting. They want to know that the candidate will not ignite a conflict but will also not run away from it. Your answer should demonstrate that you are able to work through a disagreement in a professional manner and find resolution toward a common goal.

What to Avoid:

When discussing why a co-worker was difficult to work with you should avoid insulting them or getting into too many personal details about their character. Your answer should focus more on the resolution than the individual. You should also avoid discussing tedious or irrelevant conflicts such as "she always eats my lunch from the refrigerator."

Example Response:

S/T: *In my prior role as a financial analyst, I was tasked with testing our key financial reports when updates were made to our ERP system. After a significant update, I noted that one of our accounts receivable reports was broken. The data it produced was critical to our quarterly reporting package which was due in three days. The systems analyst who managed the technical side of the financial reports was not responsive to my emails or phone calls and when I stopped by his desk to let him know the importance of fixing the report, he blew me off.*

A: *I was frustrated with his response and lack of interest in helping our team get the report fixed. However, I remained calm and requested a meeting with him to sit down for fifteen minutes to help clear the air. He apologized for not being attentive to our request and explained that he had five different projects going on and was working thirteen-hour days to keep up. We both decided it was best to schedule a meeting with him and his manager to explain our team's urgent situation and help prioritize his time.*

R: *After meeting with his manager, she was able to shuffle around some of his project work to ensure our report was fixed on time. They were both appreciative that I took the time to sit down with them to explain the situation and find a solution that worked well for everyone.*

40. WHAT ARE SOME CHARACTERISTICS OF A SUCCESSFUL TEAM?

Question Type:
Background and Personality

Question Analysis:
The interviewer will typically associate the team characteristics in in your response with your own personal working habits and gauge whether you are a good fit within their team. Your answer should focus on characteristics that align well with the company's values and are part of successful team dynamics. Some common characteristics of successful teams to consider are: effective communication, strong collaboration, diverse backgrounds and skillsets, goal driven, strong leadership, supportive, and ability to execute.

What to Avoid:

Even though it is common for teams to joke around and partake in social activities, your answer should avoid unprofessional characteristics such as "knows how to relax and have fun" or "likes to joke around."

Example Response:

Successful teams are made up of people who know how to work together to achieve a common goal. They are centered around strong leadership, effective communication and collaboration, and diverse backgrounds and skillsets. They are also goal driven and know how to complete a task.

41. ARE YOU WILLING TO WORK OVERTIME OR ON WEEKENDS IF NECESSARY?

Question Type:

Background and Personality

Question Analysis:

Even if there will be very little need to work overtime or on weekends, the interviewer will often use this question to determine the candidate's willingness to be flexible to meet the company's needs. If the company only asks an employee to work odd hours once a year for a one-off project, they want to know that the employee prioritizes their job and has a "whatever it takes" attitude to get it done. Your answer should show your willingness to work when needed but also be honest if you have limitations on your flexibility.

What to Avoid:

You should avoid going into too many unnecessary details about your personal life or commitments. You should also not commit to something if it is not feasible. Be sure to show your willingness to go above and beyond when necessary but also be open about limitations.

Example Response:

I have two young children who are involved in sports and after school activities. For a couple of their teams, I help out as an assistant coach. With that said, I am willing and able to work outside of normal hours when needed. I can be most flexible when I am notified in advance so I am able to arrange my schedule.

42. TELL ME ABOUT A TIME YOU WENT OUT OF YOUR WAY TO STRENGTHEN A CLIENT, CUSTOMER, OR TEAM MEMBER RELATIONSHIP.

Question Type:

Behavioral

Question Analysis:

Cultivating strong working relationships requires much more than a technical skillset. The interviewer will get a good sense of the candidate's interpersonal communication skills throughout the interview process, but they will use this question to find out if the candidate only focuses on their own work and objectives or if they are willing to take the time and energy to invest in internal and external working relationships. You should discuss an example that demonstrates strong soft skills and shows your willingness to go above and beyond for a co-worker or client.

What to Avoid:

You should avoid examples that would be expected under normal circumstances such as "When any of our clients send me an email, I always make sure to respond within 24 hours." You should also stay clear of examples that are not professional. "I take a new co-worker out for lunch at least once a month" is okay but it is best to avoid, "I take my team to the bar when we beat our sales numbers."

Example Response:

S: *In my previous role as a digital advertising sales representative, I led a team working on a new client project to produce twenty-five digital ads for a social media campaign. We kept our client contact updated on our work at each project milestone. As we approached the wrap up stages of the project, she surprised all of us by changing her mind and asking us to adjust the background colors and design of each ad.*

T: *Our team was frustrated because we had received positive affirmation on the ads until the very end of the project. We estimated that the edits would take an additional ten hours of work and initially considered asking the client for further payment on top of the initial project fee.*

A: *Before expressing our frustration and asking for further payment, I set up a meeting with our contact to better understand the situation. Instead of leading the conversation with our frustration, I asked about the changes and found out that it was actually her boss who changed his mind about the ads. She apologized and sympathized with the difficult situation it put us in. I told her I understood that these things happen and agreed to make the edits at no additional charge. We put in the extra work to deliver the project on time and I brought in bagels and coffee for the client and her team at the closing meeting.*

R: *Our contact was very appreciative of our hard work and willingness to go above and beyond to meet their needs. They had excellent results from the advertisements and ended up hiring us for three additional projects over the next year.*

43. TELL ME ABOUT A TIME YOU DID NOT MEET A GOAL. WHAT DID YOU LEARN?

Question Type:
Behavioral

Question Analysis:
Like the "describe a failure" question #19, you should not feel uncomfortable discussing a time you did not achieve a goal. As long as you continue to set challenging goals, you will come up short from time to time and the interviewer knows this. The

key is to be able to explain to the interviewer why you did not meet the goal and show them that you learned from it.

What to Avoid:

You should avoid placing blame on a co-worker or outside circumstances. The interviewer is looking for an example in which you take responsibility for coming up short. With that said, you should be careful not to provide an example where you failed as a result of negligence or a poor work ethic.

Example Response:

S/T: *In my prior role as a business analyst, my manager asked me to create a step-by-step visual tutorial on how to run ten different financial reports in our ERP system. She mentioned that the tutorials were urgently needed for a department project and asked me to estimate how long it would take to have it completed.*

A: *After reviewing the first couple reports I mentioned to her that I could finish all of the tutorials within two days. Shortly after, I realized I had not reviewed my calendar before making the commitment and I had four important meetings over the next two days which could not be rescheduled. To make matters worse, it quickly became evident that my estimate of time needed to complete the project was too optimistic. Initially, I had not reviewed each report; many of the tutorial sections would take much longer than expected.*

R: *I worked thirteen-hour days to try to meet the goal, but it ended up taking me four days to complete the tutorials instead of two. I took full responsibility for the delay when explaining to my manager that I had failed to consider my other obligations and did a poor job of estimating the number of hours the project would require. When setting deadlines for my work, I have learned to take the time to create a comprehensive plan that incorporates all factors and obligations. I have also learned that it is great to set challenging goals, but they should always be realistic and attainable.*

44. HOW LONG WOULD YOU PLAN TO STAY WITH THE COMPANY?

Question Type:

Ambition

Question Analysis:

Employees are not as loyal to their employers as in the past. Hiring can be a risky investment if a candidate is likely to bounce around to other companies whenever new opportunities arise. The interviewer is looking for the candidate to convince them that they are committed to the position. Your answer should focus on your enthusiasm for the opportunities within the company and position and your desire to remain with the company as long as you are continuing to grow and have a positive impact.

If you do have plans to leave town within a couple of years due to a certain circumstance (such as having a spouse in the military), be honest and upfront about it with the interviewer but if there are opportunities to work remotely, leave the door open to continue with the company.

What to Avoid:

Your answer should avoid contingencies based on promotions or pay increases such as "I'll continue to work here as long as I am paid fairly." You have not established credibility with the employer so an answer like this answer can be off-putting to the interviewer.

Example Response:

I am excited about this position but even more so about the career opportunities' working for XYZ Company. The rotational program in the marketing department enables new employees to obtain experience working in many diverse roles over their first three years with the company. I think this program would enhance my skillset and position me for future leadership roles. As long as I continue to bring value and make positive contributions, I would plan on remaining with the company.

45. IF AN URGENT WORK SITUATION CAME UP OVER THE WEEKEND, HOW WOULD YOU REACT?

Question Type:

Background and Personality

Question Analysis:

This can be a tricky question for some candidates because they interpret it as the interviewer asking if they will always be "on call." However, this is usually not the objective of the question. Instead, the interviewer wants to know that if a rare and urgent situation arose outside of normal work hours, the candidate would be willing to do whatever they could to help remediate it. You should demonstrate your willingness to help out if an urgent situation came up outside of normal work hours.

What to Avoid:

There is nothing wrong with emphasizing your belief in a work-life balance, but you should never say anything to indicate that you completely ignore work outside of the office such as "I turn my work phone off when I leave the office" or "I ignore all work communication on the weekends." On the other end of the spectrum, your answer should also not be "I make myself available at all times." The interviewer knows this is not possible.

Example Response:

I strongly believe in the benefits of finding a good work-life balance. However, the timing of urgent issues can be unpredictable. If something came up outside of work hours that required immediate attention, I would do whatever I could to help fix the problem.

46. WHAT ARE SOME WAYS YOU DEAL WITH AN UPSET CUSTOMER OR CLIENT?

Question Type:

Background and Personality

Question Analysis:

Individual interactions with vendors, clients, and customers can be reflective of the whole company. The interviewer wants to know that the candidate will be a good representative of the company, especially under pressure and difficult situations. Your answer should show that you know how to remain calm, respectful, and avoid being combative when dealing with an upset customer.

What to Avoid:

You should avoid only discussing how you **talk** to upset customers. Usually, the most important thing to do in this situation is to show the customer you are willing to **listen** to their frustration and sympathize with them. You should also avoid generic canned responses such as "my philosophy is that the customer is always right."

Example Response:

Before I try to offer any type of response or resolution, I first like to show the customer that I am willing to listen to their issue. Typically, the most effective way to calm the situation is to simply take the time to hear the customer and show sympathy for their frustration. When speaking with the customer, I am always mindful of my tone and body language to ensure I do not come across as combative. I try to come to a fair resolution and help the customer in any way I can within the company's policies. If I am not able to come to a resolution or need to look further into the problem, I take down their contact information and follow back up with them as soon as possible.

47. HOW DO YOU ENSURE QUALITY IN YOUR WORK?

Question Type:

Background and Personality

Question Analysis:

The interviewer will use this question to determine how important quality is to the candidate. They are looking for the candidate to discuss procedures they implement to ensure that their work is rooted in quality. You should emphasize your desire for quality work and discuss a process you use to ensure mistakes are limited.

What to Avoid:

The interviewer knows everyone makes mistakes, so you should avoid answers such as "I make almost no mistakes in my work." You also want to stay away from placing the burden on others with a response such as "I usually ask someone else to review my work." The interviewer is looking for you to discuss your own process to mitigate mistakes before it gets reviewed or submitted.

Example Response:

I consider myself to be an efficient worker, but I also take the time to pay close attention to detail in my work. Before I start any task, I step back to ensure I understand the full scope of the work and consider all factors. If there are questions around the deliverables, I make sure to find the answer or reach out to someone who can clarify for me. I would rather get it right the first time than have to go back and redo work. After completing my work, I always go back through it and do a detailed self-review to ensure accuracy and quality. Although I still make the occasional mistake, my process has worked well in maintaining high quality and limiting mistakes before my work gets submitted to someone else.

48. ARE YOU WILLING TO TRAVEL FOR THIS JOB?

Question Type:

Background and Personality

Question Analysis:

The interviewer will typically ask this question only when the job does require some level of travel. They are looking to confirm that the candidate has read the job description (which should indicate the amount of travel) and is agreeable with the travel requirements. Your answer should affirm that you are comfortable with the travel requirements in the job description. If the job description did not mention travel, then you should be upfront and honest about your ability to travel. Be sure to state any travel limitations during the week (such as only able to travel Mon-Fri). If you would like to learn more specifics about the travel requirements, you can find out more with a follow up question at the end of your response.

What to Avoid:

You should never tell the interviewer you are not willing to travel any less than what is stated in the job description. For example, if the description says out-of-town travel is required up to 50% of the time, you should not have applied to the job if you are only willing to travel occasionally. If you are flexible and willing to travel whenever needed, you can let the interviewer know. You should avoid discussing ulterior motives for traveling such as "I never miss a chance to get out of town for a free hotel room and free food" or "I have over 100,000 Marriott points, I would love to get more."

Example Response:

I worked as an account executive in the past and was on the road about 40% of the time. The travel did not bother me at all. When I reviewed the description for this position, it had indicated that travel would be required up to 20% of the time. However, I am flexible to travel beyond that if needed. Would the travel be during certain times of the year or more sporadic?

49. TELL ME ABOUT A TIME YOU DEALT WITH CONFLICTING PRIORITIES. HOW DID YOU DETERMINE THE TOP PRIORITY?

Question Type:

Behavioral

Question Analysis:

The interviewer will ask this question to assess the candidate's organizational and decision-making skills. Situations will often come up requiring you to organize your time to manage multiple tasks and effectively prioritize them. Your answer should demonstrate your ability to choose the top priority while not neglecting your responsibilities for the secondary priorities.

What to Avoid:

Prioritizing multiple tasks is much different than "multitasking" which infers that you work on multiple tasks at the same time. You should avoid stating that you like to multitask. Most studies show that multitasking hurts focus, sacrifices quality, and leads to less efficiency.

Example Response:

S: *In my previous position selling CRM software, my manager had signed our team up for an out-of-town two-day training event. Three hours before my flight was to depart, the contact at my largest account in the area called me frantically explaining that their software had crashed.*

T: *My manager was already on a prior flight, so I was unable to get ahold of her at the time. After considering the circumstances, I decided that the best course of action was to drive directly to the client's office to help them resolve the urgent problem.*

A: *I spent the next four hours working with the client and our IT department until the issue was resolved. I then called my manager and explained why I missed my flight and let her know that the client was very appreciative that I had made myself available right away.*

R: *My manager told me I made the right decision and said it could have been disastrous if our client had to wait longer to get the assistance they needed. I booked a later flight that evening and made it to the training on time.*

50. WHAT IS YOUR DREAM JOB?

Question Type:

Background and Personality

Question Analysis:

When this question comes up, candidates tend to focus their response on a job title instead of the attributes of a dream job. A response such as "CEO" or "CFO" will not tell the interview much aside from the candidate's desire to earn a lot of money. The interviewer will use the question to assess the candidate's goals and aspirations. You should focus your response on a job description that aligns with your strengths and ambitions. Ideally, your response is closely related to the industry or profession connected to the job for which you have applied.

What to Avoid:

You should avoid unrealistic responses such as "shortstop for the New York Yankees." The interviewer wants you to discuss a lofty but attainable position related to your career path – not your childhood aspiration. You should also avoid saying something like "this would be my dream job." The interviewer may see this response as lazy and insincere.

Example Response:

I desire to be in a position that would enable me to continue developing my graphic design and print production skills. I also have a strong interest in developing project management experience. In my dream job, I would lead a team of designers and leverage cutting-edge graphic design technology to offer innovative solutions for clients.

51. WHAT STEPS DO YOU GO THROUGH WHEN MAKING DIFFICULT DECISIONS?

Question Type:
Critical Thinking

Question Analysis:
Companies often seek candidates who possess strong critical thinking and decision-making skills. The interviewer will use this question to ensure that the candidate is able to go through

a comprehensive thought process before making a tough decision. Your response should be focused on walking through effective decision-making steps while adding clarity to each step. Be sure to walk through the decision-making steps in chronological order.

What to Avoid:
You should avoid insinuating that you make decisions too quickly or without an objective thought process. Stating something along the lines of "when faced with a difficult decision, I go with my gut instinct" is not the answer the interviewer is seeking. Instead, show the interviewer that you use an objective, evidence based approach when making tough choices.

On the other end of the spectrum, you do not want to come off as someone who overthinks all tough decisions or is too indecisive. Employers do not get value out of an employee who cannot stop second-guessing themselves. At the end of the comprehensive decision-making steps, it is beneficial to show that you are conclusive.

Example Response:
When making difficult decisions, I first define the problem or task and ensure that I fully understand the objectives.

Then, I research the important information and collect data related to the problem that will help me come up with possible solutions. When gathering information, I pay close attention to the reputation, expertise, and objectivity of the sources.

Next, I layout each of my options and consider the likelihood of the outcomes for each option.

I then make a preliminary decision and discuss the situation as well as my thought process with a trusted colleague who can provide their insight and perspective. If they concur with my decision, I move forward and execute it. If they offer contrary insight, I consider their perspective and reassess my evidence and options before making a final decision.

52. HOW DO YOU EXPAND YOUR PROFESSIONAL NETWORK?

Question Type:
Industry and Company Specific

Question Analysis:
The interviewer will ask this question because of the importance and value in building a strong internal and external professional network. Building connections within your organization means creating value, being a resource for others, and promoting collaboration. Networking externally is not just about your own career interests, it is about making connections with other organizations to identify business opportunities. Excellent ways to expand your network include: attending charity events, setting up lunches with people outside of your department, joining professional networks, and participating in internal and external trainings.

What to Avoid:

You should avoid simple and generic responses such as "I stay active on LinkedIn." Instead, try to provide specific examples of ways you expand your professional connections both internally and externally. It can be as simple as volunteering in the community or grabbing coffee with co-workers outside of your department.

Example Response:

I make it a goal to have lunch with a different co-worker from outside of my department at least once a week. I also make it a priority to make new connections through trainings, social gatherings, and volunteer events. I've found that expanding my network has created value for my organization by fostering stronger collaboration and teamwork. It's also enabled me to be a resource for those outside of my department and opened many opportunities for me within the Company.

53. HOW WOULD YOU DESCRIBE YOURSELF USING JUST ONE WORD?

Question Type:

Background and Personality

Question Analysis:

The interviewer will ask this question for two purposes. First, they want to test the candidate to see if they can follow instructions. If your answer completely ignores the question (uses more than one word to describe yourself) it can raise concerns about your listening skills. However, this does not mean your answer should be a one-word response. You should discuss why you chose a particular word to describe yourself. The interviewer will also use the question to find out more about your personality and how well it fits with the position. You should be strategic in your answer by choosing a word that compliments the job. Words that tend to fit well with a variety of positions are: dynamic, strategic, dedicated, ambitious, determined, and innovative.

What to Avoid:

You should avoid generic words that are not specific to the job such as "friendly" or "outgoing."

Example Response:

If I had to only use one word to describe myself it would be "strategic." Before starting any difficult task or project, I always set goals and develop a detailed plan to achieve those goals. I believe that in most cases being able to develop a strategic plan is just as important as the execution itself.

54. TELL ME ABOUT A TIME YOU GAVE A TEAM MEMBER CRITICAL FEEDBACK. HOW DID IT GO?

Question Type:

Behavioral

Question Analysis:

The interviewer wants to know that the candidate will not

refrain from providing critical feedback when necessary. The key to critical feedback is to ensure that it is constructive, not destructive. You should try to think of an example when you provided critical feedback to a team member but also encouraged and inspired instead of tearing them down.

What to Avoid:

You should stay away from example feedback that is critical of someone's personality or character. The feedback should be focused on their work and offer constructive solutions.

Example Response:

S/T: *In my previous job as an audit senior associate in public accounting, I was in charge of reviewing the work performed by the associates and interns on our team. We had a new associate join our team toward the end of an audit and I could tell that she felt the pressure of the large amount of work and tight deadlines we were up against. In reviewing her work, I could see that her mechanics were solid but the workpapers were sloppy with typos and small errors that should have been corrected before submitting it.*

A: *Instead of continuing to spend too much of my own time providing reviewer comments and updating her work, I decided to sit down with her to discuss the issue. When considering the associate's position in a new and demanding environment, I did not want to discourage her with my feedback. I first complimented her work in terms of her understanding and thought processes. I shared my early experiences and how I could relate to the difficultly of balancing quality and speed when under pressure to get tasks done quickly. I relayed the message that hurrying too quickly ends up taking our team even more time when we have to go back and update workpapers for typos and errors. I encouraged her to take the time to perform self-reviews before signing off on any future work.*

R: She was very receptive of my feedback and thanked me for taking the time to discuss it with her in person. After our meeting, I quickly noticed the increase in quality in her workpapers. Taking the time to offer in-person constructive feedback enabled her to make minor adjustments that have significantly improved her work.

55. TELL ME ABOUT A TIME YOU HAD TO DISCUSS BAD NEWS WITH A CUSTOMER OR CLIENT. HOW DID IT GO?

Question Type:
Behavioral

Question Analysis:
This is a common question when interviewing for a leadership position or a role with heavy interaction with outside customers. The interviewer will use the question to assess the candidate's ability to communicate effectively with a customer under challenging circumstances. When drawing on a past situation, it is important to choose one in which you were honest and forthright while also acknowledging the negative impact of the news to the customer. Ideally, your example has

action items that were taken to resolve an issue or includes some other positive takeaways.

What to Avoid:

You should avoid sounding like you sugar coat bad news. While it is good to empathize with their situation, it makes the circumstance even worse if you are not direct in your communication.

Example Response:

S: In my previous role as a senior tax associate, our firm took on a project to perform a research and development tax analysis for a local client. I was tasked with leading the project and submitting our work to my manager before it would be presented to the client.

T: The client had their own tax deadlines coming up, so I assessed the work and let them know that we could wrap up the project within two weeks. One week into the project, I was notified that our largest client in the area had an unexpected and urgent tax issue come up which would require the immediate attention of everyone in our office.

A: I knew that informing my client that our project would be late would not be well received because they were up against their own deadlines and I had promised to have it completed on time. I scheduled an in-person meeting with my main contact at the client and explained that we had an urgent and unanticipated issue come up which would pull our team away from the project for the next two weeks. I told her that I understood her frustration and that I would feel the same way if I were in her shoes. I then asked her what she thought about me transitioning the remaining work to another one of our firm's offices to try to meet the deadline. She was perfectly okay with transitioning the work to a different team provided the quality of the work remained consistent.

R: I received approval from my manager to reach out to another office within our firm and ended up finding personnel who had worked on similar projects in the past. I was able to coordinate with them to ensure the remaining work was completed by the deadline. I reviewed the work in detail before submitting it to my manager and the client. Our client contact was very happy with the results of the project and she thanked me afterwards for finding a solution that worked out well for everyone.

56. HOW DO YOU HELP DRIVE INNOVATION?

Question Type:
Background and Personality

Question Analysis:
In today's economy, technology has enabled change and innovation faster than at any other time in history. Employers consistently rank the ability to innovate as a top trait sought after in candidates. Interviewers will use this question to assess the candidate's mentality on innovation and find out what

techniques they use to contribute to it. Common ways to drive innovation include: cross functional collaboration, challenging current processes, setting vision based goals, and embracing continuing education.

What to Avoid:

Innovation is achieved through a calculated process, not a spontaneous event. You should avoid discussing innovative actions without discussing the process behind them. Companies value calculated innovation, but they do not benefit from spontaneous change.

Example Response:

To survive and grow in today's economy, companies need to create a culture of innovation. Innovation is not just about creating new goods and services, it is also about adding value by improving existing systems and processes. I believe that opportunities for innovation arise most often when employees embrace the right mindset and work habits. I find those opportunities by setting ambitious goals, constantly challenging the processes behind my work, collaborating with other functions and departments, and not being afraid to take calculated risks when there is opportunity to improve.

57. WHAT IS THE BEST COURSE OF ACTION WHEN A SUPERIOR ASKS YOU TO DO SOMETHING UNETHICAL?

Question Type:

Background and Personality

Question Analysis:

This question will come up often in professions that rely heavily on ethical integrity. The interviewer wants to obtain a better understanding of how the candidate will respond in a difficult situation involving ethics. Your response should demonstrate that you will not act on impulse and will thoroughly consider the facts and circumstances before taking appropriate action.

What to Avoid:

This situation requires many considerations and a well thought out response. Be sure to avoid an oversimplified and impulsive answer such as "immediately report them to the Board of Directors!"

Example Response:

I believe that trust, respect, and loyalty are key components of all successful working relationships with bosses. However, being asked to do something unethical or illegal would be a violation of trust and respect, and loyalty would not be a top concern. Before taking any course of action, I would consider the surrounding facts and circumstances of the situation as well as the potential impact of what they were asking me to do. If I still had concerns about the ethics of the situation, I would first speak directly with that person to discuss those concerns. If there was no resolution and they continued to pressure me or threatened disciplinary action, I would contact the company's ethics hotline. If there was not an ethics hotline option, I would consult with the HR department.

58. HOW DO YOU DEMONSTRATE LEADERSHIP?

Question Type:
Background and Personality

Question Analysis:
Questions around leadership come up often during interviews. Even if the job is not for a management position, strong leadership skills are essential for all candidates. The interviewer is looking for the candidate to explain some of their leadership traits and provide an example of how they have used those traits to be an effective leader. Some strong leadership characteristics you can consider in your response are: Effective communicator, taking initiative, making difficult decisions, motivating those around you, and empowering team members.

What to Avoid:
You should avoid telling the interviewer that you have not yet had the opportunity to lead people. It is okay if you have not been in an official leadership role in the past. You can reference any task or project (possibly from college) or a volunteer opportunity where you stepped up to make decisions that impacted the rest of the group.

Example Response:

I demonstrate leadership by clearly communicating goals, objectives, and expectations up front with team members. I also empower those around me by challenging them to present their own ideas that can bring value to the team. Finally, I believe in leading by example. I would never expect team members to do something one way when I am contradicting that through my own actions.

I was president of the student marketing association on campus my senior year and we set lofty fundraising goals to fund our annual trip to New York. The organization had come up short in prior years and I did not want that to happen while I was president. I communicated our goals and expectations to the members well in advance of the fundraising period and I encouraged members to share new ideas to raise additional funding. Through our collaboration, we ended up implementing two additional fundraising events and surpassed our goal for the annual trip. Encouraging collaboration and developing a detailed and achievable plan was key to our success.

59. WHAT RESOURCES DO YOU USE TO KEEP UP WITH CHANGES TO THE INDUSTRY?

Question Type:

Industry and Company Specific

Question Analysis:

Most industries are constantly evolving through new laws, regulations, research, best practices, and technology. The interviewer will use this question to see if the candidate has taken the initiative to keep up with news and changes in the industry. Most industries offer subscriptions to journals or publications. Professional training, continuing education, professional organizations, and online outlets offer other opportunities to keep up with an industry. If you have not yet leveraged any of these options, the quickest and most convenient way to do so before the interview is to visit a few online sites and publications.

What to Avoid:

You should avoid any answer that insinuates you do not care about keeping up with the industry, such as "I'm so busy with my work that I do not have much time to keep up with industry related news." It is okay if you have not had the chance to join a professional organization or take continuing education. You can still take the time to visit online resources and highlight those in your response. You can also emphasize your desire to leverage some of the other options.

Example Response:

I frequently read articles on the "Modern Marketing Today" website as well as the marketing section of the Forbes website. I also subscribe to the Wall Street journal which frequently has excellent writeups on the marketing industry. I especially like reading about new research and technology advances that are opening new opportunities in the industry. I have also started to look into becoming a member with the American Marketing Association and plan to attend some of their live events in the future.

60. ARE YOU AN EFFECTIVE LISTENER?

Question Type:

Communication

Question Analysis:

Being a good listener is an essential skill for just about every job. Interviewers will usually be able to tell if the candidate is a good listener throughout the interview. They will often use this question to see if the candidate recognizes the traits of an effective listener. Your answer should include some of the methods you use when listening to others.

What to Avoid:

Your answer should not be a simple "yes, I am" to this question. The interviewer is not looking for a long drawn out answer here, but you should be sure to discuss how you listen. Although it may seem creative, this is not the time to pull off a joke by responding with "What did you say?"

Example Response:

I do consider myself an effective listener. When people communicate with me, I listen intently and give them the time to deliver their thoughts before responding. I ensure that I maintain eye contact while they are speaking and provide non-verbal messages such as nodding when they emphasize a point.

If I am not positive about something they said, I confirm my understanding by paraphrasing or asking questions before I respond.

61. IN YOUR ESTIMATION, HOW MANY TURKEYS ARE SOLD ANNUALLY IN THE UNITED STATES FOR EACH THANKSGIVING?

Question Type:

Critical Thinking

Question Analysis:

Interviewers will ask these types of questions to assess the candidate's critical thinking skills and ability to use logic and reasoning on the spot. You may not receive this exact question but a similar structured question to the one above is not uncommon. Too often candidates get worried about coming up with an accurate number. It is important to remember that the answer does not matter nearly as much as the thought process. Your answer should walk the interviewer through the logic you used to arrive at your answer.

What to Avoid:

You should avoid simply providing a number without the reasoning in your response. There are variables that the interviewer would not expect you to know to arrive at the answer. Therefore, your focus should emphasize your thought process over accuracy to demonstrate your critical thinking ability to the interviewer.

Example Response:

I estimate that there are around 320 million people in the United States and the average family size is four. If each family purchased one turkey, this would come out to about 8 million turkeys. However, I am estimating that about 10% of families choose to eat something other than turkey so that would be about 7.2 million turkeys sold each thanksgiving.

62. HOW DO YOU HANDLE STRESS ON THE JOB?

Question Type:
Background and Personality

Question Analysis:
Stress comes along with most jobs these days. The interviewer will use this question to see how you react to stressful situations. They would like to discern that you take stressful situations seriously but also remain calm, cool, and collected. Your answer should include an example of how you handled a stressful situation in the past.

What to Avoid:
You should avoid unrealistic responses such as "I never get stressed." The interviewer knows that everyone occasionally experiences stress. When providing an example, your answer should not focus on the degree of your stress but more on how

you reacted to it in a positive way. You should also be careful not to insinuate that you get stressed in common situations that would be applicable to the job such as "meeting with a client." The example should be a unique and relatable situation.

Example Response:

When faced with stress over something like a tight deadline, I like to assess the situation and come up with a detailed plan before taking further action. Too often, people let the stress consume them and they immediately focus on the execution instead of the planning. This can often lead to lower quality work and take even more time when work needs to be redone.

I recently had a client inform me that they had an urgent situation come up and needed to move a project due date up two weeks. Our team had not even started the project as we were not expecting to deliver it any time soon. We all felt a sense of stress and panic when we heard the news. Instead of frantically diving right into the project work, I set up a meeting for the whole team to plan out the tasks in detail and lay out a time line. Our detailed plan helped us envision a path to success and execute our tasks. We ended up delivering the project on time and the client was very satisfied with our work.

63. TELL ME ABOUT A TIME WHEN YOU MOTIVATED OTHERS AROUND YOU.

Question Type:

Behavioral

Question Analysis:

This is a common question when interviewing for managerial positions or when the candidate will be working in project leadership roles or with outside customers or clients. The interviewer is looking to assess the candidate's leadership capabilities. Before discussing how you motivate others around you, it is important to acknowledge that people respond to different motivators based on their personality and work style. You should consider an example that includes effective motivation methods, such as: recognition of achievements, consistent feedback, clear and concise communication, and incentive-based rewards.

What to Avoid:

You should avoid discussing overly-aggressive tactics that would put too much pressure on those around you. The interviewer is looking for motivational techniques that encourage not intimidate. You should also be careful not to overemphasize incentive based motivation. Unless you will be working with a commissioned sales team, you do not want to set a precedent of always providing a tangible reward when someone does the work they are expected to do.

Example Response:

S/T: *In my previous role as a project manager, I lead a group of three other programmers to upgrade our CRM system. As the leader on a critical project for the company, I wanted to ensure my co-workers were motivated to meet the tight deadlines and provide their best work.*

A: *One programmer was a new hire and I could tell that he really wanted to make a great impression on the project but often questioned his work and assumptions. I decided to meet with him twice a week to provide him consistent feedback on his work. The meetings also offered him the opportunity to run through his questions with me. After a few meetings of offering both positive and constructive feedback, I noticed his confidence in his work began to increase.*

A: *The second programmer on the project was more experienced and her work was excellent, but she tended to be reserved in team situations. I decided to stop by her desk frequently to recognize her great work throughout the project. I could tell she really appreciated the recognition and I noticed that she started to become more vocal in our team meetings.*

A: *The last co-worker had been with the company over five years and had been seeking leadership opportunities. I met with him early on in the project and offered him the opportunity to lead some of our team meetings and help coach other team members. I also offered to provide a positive review to his manager based upon his success affirming his leadership role on the project. He embraced the leadership opportunities and was instrumental in the success of the project.*

R: *Our team did an excellent job on the project and we completed it ahead of the schedule. I believe that understanding my co-worker's personalities and needs was essential to providing them with the right motivation.*

64. WHAT ACCOMPLISHMENT ARE YOU MOST PROUD OF?

Question Type:

Background and Personality or Behavioral

Question Analysis:

The interviewer will often use this question to learn more about your background, interests, and values. Ideally, your answer will convey personal traits that align well with the skills needed for the position. For example, if the job calls for the candidate to possess strong attention to detail or team communication skills, you can use an example that exemplifies these traits. If you provide a work setting example, you can treat this as a behavioral question and use the STAR method to respond. At the conclusion, be sure to explain why the accomplishment was so important to you.

What to Avoid:

It is usually best to avoid personal accomplishments that have nothing to do with your professional skills or experience. If you do use a personal accomplishment, be sure to emphasize some professional skills (such as team collaboration) that were used to achieve the accomplishment. You also want to avoid answers that are too short or simple. These types of responses will undermine your accomplishments. You should not hold back on showing enthusiasm and pride in your accomplishment.

Example Response:

S/T: *The college I attended understood the value in preparing business students to use ERP software, including SAP. In addition to the ERP focused courses during the year, they also brought in a certified SAP instructor during the summer to offer a two-week boot camp for those who wanted to become certified in SAP. The course lasted ten hours each day and covered over 1,000 pages of material which culminated in a four-hour exam. The pass rates were only about 50%. I knew that passing the course would open the door to many more professional opportunities, but my SAP experience was limited at the time, so it seemed like a daunting task.*

A: *We had not even made it through day three of the course and I already felt like I was drowning in the content. When class let out on the first couple days, I had gone home at night to study independently but after day three, I decided to speak with a few class members about creating a collaborative study group on campus. I developed a robust study plan to ensure we covered the most important topics each evening until the day of the final exam. We assigned each member to be an expert in one of the topics. As a result, they were equipped to lead the group discussions in their area and assist others in the group when specific questions came up.*

R: *It was an incredibly demanding two-week period, but each member of the group went on to pass the exam and I ended up with the best score in the whole class. I was most proud of the way we worked together as a group to plan, collaborate, and execute. Each of us in the group ended up leveraging our success* *from that course to open the door to many great career opportunities.*

65. TELL ME ABOUT A TIME YOU USED LOGIC AND CRITICAL THINKING TO SOLVE A PROBLEM. WHAT WAS THE OUTCOME?

Question Type:
Behavioral

Question Analysis:
Most employers rank critical thinking and problem-solving skills at the top of their list for desired traits in applicants. Excellent methods to show strong critical thinking skills include: analyzing the factors surrounding the problem, considering the options and their likely outcomes, developing a plan, and executing the most favorable solution.

What to Avoid:
You should avoid examples that are not strongly correlated to the job description. For instance, if you are interviewing for a technical engineering role that has no contact with outside customers, you would typically not want to discuss solving a problem for an upset customer in a customer service role unless the problem itself was technical in nature and related to engineering.

Example Response:
S: *In my prior position as a procurement analyst, I performed*

an assessment of our $100,000+ raw material inventory purchases for the year which all went through an approval process. My analysis showed that it was taking an average of 15 days to get the $100,000+ purchases through two manager approvals and one VP approval. I also determined that any customer order which required materials from a $100,000+ inventory purchase slowed our manufacturing lead time down by that same average of 15 days.

T: Our team agreed that the long approval process and increased manufacturing lead time was negatively impacting our customers. I decided to analyze options to reduce the approval process and present them to my manager.

A: The first option I considered was to update the approval process to bypass the two manager approvals and go directly to the VP. However, I determined that the managers were more closely involved in the day-to-day warehouse operations and the VP found value in having their approvals and input before approving the purchases. Next, I considered updating the approval threshold to $200,000+ since historical data showed 75% of the inventory purchases above $100,000 would fall below $200,000. However, the company made it a priority to implement measures to mitigate risk and the upper level managers sought visibility into all significant operational decisions. The last option I considered was to implement a new approval system that gave the approvers deadlines of two days and enabled them to input a replacement approver in their *queue when they were traveling or too busy to approve the purchase. I decided to recommend this third option because it kept the three-level review system in place but used effective measures to significantly speed up the process.*

R: My manager agreed with my assessment and we implemented the new approval system. Within three months of the implementation, the average approval process dropped from 15 days to 5. We also started to receive comments from our sales team about a noticeable increase in customer satisfaction as a result of our reduction in delivery time.

66. DO YOU TEND TO BE A LEADER OR FOLLOWER?

Question Type:
Background and Personality

Question Analysis:
This can be a tricky question because many candidates assume that the correct answer is "leader" but in reality, the interviewer is usually looking for the candidate to be capable of being both a leader and a follower. Being versatile enough to be a strong leader or follower will provide the interviewer positive affirmation that the candidate will fit in well with the company. In your response, you should use examples to demonstrate that you can be either a leader or follower, depending on the situation.

What to Avoid:

You should avoid stating that you are "always a leader." Even managers and executives need to be able to be effective followers in certain circumstances. If you are in an entry level position, you should also avoid saying you are "always a follower." There will be tasks and projects that will require you to take on a leadership role and the interviewer will want to be confident that you have the capability to lead.

Example Response:

Depending on the circumstances, I am effective at being either a leader or a follower.

In my prior role as a financial analyst, I was informed that an unexpected transaction occurred which would require me to make complicated adjustments to our year-end forecast. We were up against a tight deadline, so my manager sat down with me to explain the changes I would need to make to the forecast. Normally, I would want to understand more detail about the transaction before making the adjustments. However, with the deadline in mind, my priority was to take detailed notes during the meeting with my manager and follow through on everything she asked me to change.

In my current role as a senior business analyst, the project manager on a system implementation asked me to lead the financial component of the project. I embraced the leadership role and managed a team of four financial analysts through the end of the two-month project. After a successful implementation, the project manager complimented me on my leadership and organizational skills.

67. ARE YOU A SELF-MOTIVATED?

Question Type:
Ambition

Question Analysis:
Interviewers will use this question to assess the candidate's drive and passion from a professional standpoint. Employers seek workers who excel independently without the need for constant guidance and supervision. Your answer should focus on your enthusiasm and drive to succeed. This is an excellent opportunity to include an example that demonstrates your self-motivation.

What to Avoid:
You should be careful not to insinuate that you find your work boring and therefore require the use of motivational tactics to get through the day. An answer such as "I set up a countdown clock to the weekend to help me get through the week" will not go over well with the interviewer. Instead, try to show the interviewer that you take pride in the accomplishment and outcome of your work.

Example Response:
I have always been a self-motivated person. I take pride in producing quality work and coming up with solutions to difficult challenges. I am strong at setting goals, developing

plans, and executing my work to achieve those goals. My passion and drive for this profession lead me to join the board of the local marketing association three years ago and I was recently voted in as the treasurer.

68. HOW DO YOU PREPARE FOR PRESENTATIONS?

Question Type:

Communication

Question Analysis:

The ability to effectively present information to an audience or small group is an important skill for most positions. Even entry level positions typically require an occasional presentation to co-workers or management. The interviewer will use this question to get a feel for how comfortable the candidate is as a presenter and assess their knowledge on effective techniques to prepare for a presentation. Best presentation preparation practices include: defining the objectives, incorporating visual aids, practicing out loud, time management, and rehearsing in front of others.

What to Avoid:

You should avoid stating that you have no experience giving presentations. If your only experience is from college, you can still discuss the methods you used to prepare. Remember that the emphasis is on the preparation techniques. There is really no need to wrapped up in discussing a specific example of a presentation, especially if your only presentation experience came from outside of a professional setting.

Example Response:

Before preparing a presentation, I like to first define my objectives and create a detailed outline of the material that will achieve them. I find that including graphs, charts, and other visual aids in my presentation help me reinforce my talking points and keep the audience engaged. Once my presentation is put together, I practice it aloud and keep track of how much time I am spending on each section to help make necessary adjustments. I then practice my speech in front of family or friends and gather their feedback. By the time I give the real presentation, I usually feel calm and confident because I have already practiced it 3 or 4 times.

69. WHAT IS YOUR CURRENT SALARY?

Question Type:
Background and Personality

Question Analysis:
The interviewer will ask this question to get a feeling for what type of compensation package the candidate would be seeking before accepting a potential job offer. They will often use the candidate's current salary as a baseline and make a higher offer with the amount depending on the responsibilities that come with the new job. While I do not recommend providing your actual salary information to third party recruiters, once you

reach the interview phase, you should be upfront and honest about your pay. Be sure to include bonuses, incentive pay, overtime, and commissions in your response.

What to Avoid:

You should avoid anything but an honest straightforward answer to this question. Refusing to disclose your salary or providing an indirect response will only hurt your chances for a job offer.

Example Response:

My current salary is $52,500 but I am also eligible for a 10% performance bonus which I have received each of the past two years.

70. DO YOU TAKE WORK HOME WITH YOU?

Question Type:

Background and Personality

Question Analysis:

Before developing an answer to this question, it is important to consider the nature of the profession as well as the company's culture. Some companies seek a culture of highly efficient employees who are focused on completing their work in the office. Other companies, such as law and accounting firms, seek employees who are accessible outside of the office and are willing to plug back into work when needed. Ideally, your preferences and answer will align closely with the company's culture while showing you are willing to be flexible when the situation calls for it.

What to Avoid:

You should avoid hardline responses such as "I never take my work home" or "I work from home every night."

Example Response:

I typically go through my task list at the beginning of each week and budget my time to allow myself to complete my work at the office. However, sometimes items come up or tasks take longer than expected. I am always willing to bring my work home to meet my deadlines and the needs of the team.

71. HOW WOULD YOUR CLOSE FRIENDS DESCRIBE YOU?

Question Type:

Background and Personality

Question Analysis:

The interviewer will use this question to find out more about the candidate's personality. By asking how your friends would describe you, the question disconnects you from your own perception and forces you to consider the perception of others who are close to you. You should discuss personality traits that would be beneficial to the job and try to provide examples of exhibiting them in the setting of your friends. Traits that are relevant to a wide range of positions include: dependable, strong communicator, loyal, leader, and persistent.

What to Avoid:

You should avoid discussing traits that would not be relevant to the position such as "my friends would describe me as the life of the party." You should also avoid discussing traits that are too specific to the position such as "my friends would say that I am excellent at analyzing computer code." Unless you and your friends really do write code for fun, this will come off to the interviewer as a disingenuous response.

Example Response:

My close friends would say that I am dependable and persistent. They know when I make a commitment they can always count on me to deliver. They also know that when I am faced with a challenge, I do not give up until I find a solution. Last year, a close friend volunteered to lead a fundraiser for underprivileged children in the area and asked me to help coordinate the event. The night before the fundraiser, the weather forecast showed a large thunderstorm moving in the next day which threatened the outdoor event. We had a few hours to find a new solution or cancel the event all together. I immediately reached out to community and business leaders in the area to try to find an indoor venue. I was eventually able to get a hold of the President of the local Chamber of Commerce and she graciously offered to let us use a local banquet hall for free. We communicated the change of venue to the RSVP list and the fundraiser ended up being a success.

72. HOW DO YOU DEAL WITH A BAD DAY AT WORK?

Question Type:

Background and Personality

Question Analysis:

The interviewer will use this question to find out how the candidate responds to adversity. In demanding positions, most people will experience days when it seems like everything goes wrong. Your answer should show the interviewer that you are able to maintain a positive mindset and be a persistent problem solver in the face of challenging issues.

What to Avoid:

A bad day at work usually implies work challenges that will need to be overcome. Your answer should avoid discussing a reaction that, by itself, suggests defeat such as "I try to forget about it and start fresh the next day." It is okay to discuss getting your mind off of work after a bad day, but the answer should include your focus on positivity and resilience to tackle the outstanding challenges.

Example Response:

When it seems like everything went wrong at work, I like to turn my attention elsewhere for a couple of hours. I'll either go to the gym or grab a beer at a local tavern to relax. Shifting my focus away from work for a little while helps me clear my mind and feel rejuvenated. I then turn my focus back on the issues that caused me to have a bad day and consider action items I can take the following day to work toward resolutions. I find that clearing my mind and going to sleep with a game plan in place helps me shake off the bad day and come back with confidence to face any outstanding challenges.

73. ARE YOU A RISK TAKER?

Question Type:
Background and Personality

Question Analysis:
Candidates often think of risk as a bad thing but in reality, anyone who makes decisions on the job needs to be comfortable with some level of risk. The interviewer is not looking for an absolute answer to this question, they are using it to see if the candidate has a solid grasp on the nature of risk in a professional environment. The key to a successful answer is to explain that you avoid unnecessary risks but when necessary, you are comfortable relying on objective information and data to take calculated risks.

What to Avoid:
You typically do not want to respond with an absolute "no" answer to this question, unless you are interviewing for a specific job that requires virtually zero decision-making skills. Most positions require some decisions to be based on risk. When explaining your position on taking risks, be sure to avoid responses such as "I have excellent gut instincts." You want to demonstrate that you use reliable data to make impartial decisions. The interviewer will typically avoid hiring candidates who take a subjective approach to risk.

Example Response:

I avoid unnecessary risks; however, most professionals will occasionally find themselves in situations when they need to make decisions with incomplete information. I am comfortable taking risks as long as they are calculated. I still want to be reasonably sure of the outcome. When collecting data for a decision-making process, I place a strong emphasis on the reliability of the sources to ensure the data is accurate. I also confer with a trusted colleague when the decision merits a second perspective.

74. HOW DO YOU DEFINE SUCCESS?

Question Type:

Background and Personality

Question Analysis:

Similar to question #26, candidates can be caught off guard with this question because it is very broad. However, there is no need to overthink it or get philosophical in your answer. The interviewer is typically looking for a response about success in the workplace. They will often use the question to get a better understanding of your personality and work ethic.

What to Avoid:

You should generally avoid getting personal or philosophical with this question. Instead, try to define success in a way that depicts your personality as a professional and aligns well with the company's values.

Example Response:

Success to me is achieving goals through hard work and integrity. Before I do most tasks, I establish goals. Even if it is as simple as telling myself I will complete a simple task within the next hour. I find success through defining my goals, developing a plan to accomplish the goals, and executing my plan to achieve the desired results.

75. WHAT IS THE BEST WAY FOR A NEW EMPLOYEE TO ESTABLISH CREDIBILITY?

Question Type:

Background and Personality

Question Analysis:

The interviewer will use this question to gauge how important it is to the candidate to establish themselves as a trusted and respected co-worker within the company. They will also assess the response to see how well the candidate would fit in with the team. Your answer should emphasize your eagerness to take the initiative to learn from other employees, understand the business, and embrace personal responsibility.

What to Avoid:

Your answer should avoid insinuating that you will come in right away and make big fixes or changes to impress your co-workers. Those who try to initiate quick changes without first fully understanding the business usually do more harm than good. Instead, focus on your willingness to learn from your co-workers before taking action.

Example Response:

To establish credibility, I would first focus on learning as much as I could from my teammates. I would set up meetings with them to ask questions that would help me better understand their roles within the organization and how we would be working together. I would emphasize the value I would put on having them as a resource when working through my tasks. I would also be sure to demonstrate that I am dependable and embrace personal responsibility. It's a big turnoff when people try to deflect blame or make excuses, even when they are brand new to an organization.

76. TELL ME ABOUT A TIME YOU HAD TO EXPLAIN SOMETHING COMPLEX TO SOMEONE WHO DID NOT HAVE TECHNICAL KNOWLEDGE IN THE AREA. HOW DID IT GO?

Question Type:
Behavioral

Question Analysis:
In most roles, it is important to be able to effectively convey information to those outside of your team or department. The interviewer wants to know that you have the capability to tailor your message to suit the individual or audience you are speaking

to. In your response, you should consider focusing on the methods you commonly use to simplify complex information for your audience. Some excellent methods include: walking through scenarios or examples of how the concept works and focusing the dialogue on the components that are most relevant and applicable to the audience.

If you feel stuck with this question, think back to a time you trained someone on the job, gave a presentation to a group who was not familiar with the details of the topic, or explained a new concept to a person or group in an academic setting.

What to Avoid:

The "complex" example does not need to be rocket science, but it should also not be something that only takes thirty seconds to explain such as "I showed my new co-worker how to enter her time in our payroll system." Your answer should not simply be "I explained, and they understood..." It should emphasize the methods you used to simplify the information.

Example Response:

S: *In my previous role as a financial analyst, I provided written analysis of the results of our monthly financial statements to the vice president of investor relations. One period, we had a large foreign exchange loss flow through our income statement from our Malaysian entity. My commentary for the period explained that the loss was due to a large movement in the foreign currency which impacted the income statement due to the fact that our functional currency was the USD at that location.*

T: *The VP did not grasp the accounting rules around functional currency and emailed me asking for more information.*

A: *Instead of emailing back and simply pointing to the technical accounting guidance, I scheduled a meeting to walk through his questions in more detail. I put together a brief PowerPoint presentation that included easy-to-follow example transactions to show him how the accounting rules impacted the financial statements.*

R: *By the end of our meeting, I could see that the light bulb went on for him. He was very appreciative that I took the time to walk him through the complex accounting treatment. He even notified me later on that he used my presentation when answering questions from the investor community.*

77. WHAT DO YOU KNOW ABOUT OUR COMPETITION?

Question Type:
Industry and Company Specific

Question Analysis:
The interviewer will use this question to assess how well the candidate understands the company and its industry. Being able to identify the competition typically requires research beyond the basic information on the company's website. You do not need to spend hours doing extensive research, but you should be

able to discuss a couple of the company's products or services and how they differ from the competition. You should also be able to discuss how the company's market share compares to its competitors.

What to Avoid:

You should avoid generic statements such as "I know this company dominates its competition." An answer like this will only tell the interviewer you have not done your homework. If the company is not an industry leader, you should avoid statements that make them sound bad such as "I know that this company only has a 5% share of the market." You should instead focus on the positive aspects of your research. An example would be "I know that this company has approximately 5% of the market share in the industry and is focused on expanding its customer base by being an industry leader in product innovation."

Example Response:

I know that this company is the leader in the office furniture industry with a 25% market share. Its closest competitor is XZY Company whose top selling product is the XZY office chair. I've read that the competitors in the industry keep attempting to produce an office chair with similar ergonomics to this company's industry leading XYZ chair, but so far, they have been unsuccessful. While this company provides value to the market through quality and innovation, many of its competitors try to pick up market share through offering lower priced options.

78. HOW DO YOU MAINTAIN THE CONFIDENTIALITY OF SENSITIVE INFORMATION?

Question Type:
Background and Personality

Question Analysis:
Interviewers will typically ask this question when the position involves some level of safeguarding confidential information. Whether it is health records, client data, social security numbers, employee salaries, non-public financial information, banking numbers, patented formulas, or any other private data, a company takes on a lot of risk by handling this type of information. They need to be positive they can trust their employees to keep it safe and confidential. You should emphasize how important it is to you to protect sensitive information and discuss some best practices or an example of safeguarding data from your prior experience.

What to Avoid:
All candidates will say they are careful with sensitive information, but this response is not enough. The interviewer is looking for the candidate to discuss examples of how they protect sensitive information.

Example Response:
In the digital age, the amount of risk taken on when handling confidential information cannot be overemphasized. I treat

confidential information with the same level of respect and protection as my own social security number. I never discuss or handle it outside of the boundaries of its intended use.

I believe that all employees should be intimately familiar with their company's policies on sensitive information and keep a close eye on how technology impacts it. If I handle sensitive information on my computer, I make it a habit to always lock it with a password when I am away from my desk. If I will be viewing sensitive information on my computer and my screen is visible to those around me, I like to use a privacy screen protector. I also check with the IT department regularly to ensure I have the best available security software on my computer.

79. TELL ME ABOUT A TIME YOUR TEAM UNDERWENT CHANGE. HOW DID YOU RESPOND?

Question Type:

Behavioral

Question Analysis:

Personnel changes occur regularly in most companies, especially in leadership positions. The interviewer will use this question to ensure that the candidate is comfortable with adapting to a rapidly changing environment. You should focus your response around how your actions brought value to your team during a transition period.

What to Avoid:

You should avoid insignificant changes such as "Lauren transitioned the customer service calls over to me." Under most circumstances, an ideal example would be a leadership change within your team.

Example Response:

S: *In my prior role as a financial analyst, our team manager, Mary, accepted a two-year assignment to relocate to our business in China. Our company had a difficult time finding her replacement so by the time the new manager started, Mary had already left the country for her new role.*

T: *The new manager received limited training from our finance director, so it was communicated to our team that we would largely be responsible for training him on our current systems and processes.*

A: *At that time, I was the most experienced member on our team, so I decided to schedule a team meeting to discuss a plan to initiate our new manager. During the meeting, I recommended that each team member create a high-level summary of their areas of responsibility and corresponding tasks. After the summaries were created, I consolidated the information into one organized file and sent it to the new manager. I then requested his approval to ask each team member to schedule one-on-one meetings to walk him through their tasks and processes. With so much new information to absorb, I felt that it would be most effective for him to learn one meeting at a time over the first couple months instead of bombarding him in a disorganized fashion.*

R: *Our manager ended up having a smooth transition into the new role and pointed out to our team that his early success was largely due to our planning and accommodations.*

80. HAVE YOU EVER HAD TO FIRE SOMEONE? HOW DID IT GO? IF NOT, HOW WOULD IT GO?

Question Type:

Behavioral

Question Analysis:

This question comes up frequently for those interviewing for managerial positions. It also comes up for candidates who will be in positions that can transition into management. The interviewer will use the question to ensure the candidate is capable of dismissing someone but only when it is carefully considered and absolutely necessary. You should demonstrate in your answer you would consider other options first but, if necessary, would handle it in a professional manner.

What to Avoid:

In your example, you should avoid heavily criticizing the person you had to fire; especially through personal attacks. You should also try to avoid discussing instances when firing someone is the only reasonable action such as "we caught Susie stealing from the company." The purpose of the question is to discuss a situation which would require thoughtful consideration before making the decision.

Example Response:

S: *In a previous position, I was the manager of a sales team that sold printers and other office supplies to local businesses. We had a new sales associate named Brad on our team who was struggling to keep up with his sales quotas.*

T: *I scheduled frequent meetings with Brad to offer encouragement and discuss the challenges he was facing. Based on our discussions, I had a sense that he did not have a strong inherent drive to succeed in sales. After many consecutive months of underperformance, I asked our top sales representative to let Brad shadow him for a week to learn his best practices. When Brad declined the offer, I knew I was not left with many other options than to let him go.*

A: *I sat down with Brad and explained that I saw a lot of potential in him as a professional, but sales did not seem to be his passion. I told him that we would be letting him go but he could stay on for two weeks and help around the office while he looked for a new opportunity elsewhere.*

R: *Brad agreed with me that the experience taught him his interest was not in sales. Over the next two weeks I connected him with those in our other departments and he had the opportunity to shadow some of their work. Through that experience he developed an interest in digital marketing and took the next steps to pursue that career path.*

81. WHAT WAS YOUR FAVORITE COURSE IN COLLEGE? WHY?

Question Type:
Background and Personality

Question Analysis:
The interviewer will commonly use this question as a way to gauge the candidate's level of interest in the profession. If their favorite course had nothing to do with the job, it can raise red flags about their long-term passion and commitment to the industry. Your answer should associate interest and skills from the course to those that are relevant to the job.

What to Avoid:
If possible, avoid discussing a course that has nothing to do with the job or profession. If your favorite course was an elective such as "art history" but you are interviewing for a finance role, you can say, "My favorite finance course in college was..." At least then you will be able to discuss information that pertains to the job. If the interviewer presses you and follows up with, "That was your favorite finance course but what about your overall favorite?" You should be honest and explain why you enjoyed art history so much.

Example Response:
My favorite finance course in college was Corporate Financial Management. The course applied many of the financial theories and calculations I had learned in previous courses to

real case studies. The professor had a hands-on approach, letting us work through realistic scenarios using data and calculations such as the internal rate of return to recommend decisions that would have a significant impact on the company. I received an A in the course and enjoyed it so much that I decided to pursue a career in corporate finance.

82. DO YOU PREFER WRITTEN OR VERBAL COMMUNICATION?

Question Type:

Communication

Question Analysis:

This is somewhat of a trick question because there is no right or wrong answer here. In fact, the interviewer is typically looking for the candidate to stay away from stating a strong preference for one over the other because they can both be preferable, depending on the situation. Your answer should illustrate your ability to identify the most effective approach, and highlight your preference for utilizing either method, depending upon the situation.

What to Avoid:

Your answer should avoid stating a strong preference for one line of communication over the other. You should also avoid an oversimplified answer such "I like verbal and written communication equally."

Example Response:

I prefer the line of communication that is most effective for the given situation. For simple non-urgent requests or questions, I prefer email or an office messenger application. For matters that are more complicated or require back and forth dialogue, I prefer to use email to request an in-person meeting. If I have a quick question for a co-worker and the answer will help me move forward with what I'm working on, I'll either hop on the phone and give them a call or stop by their desk to discuss it. As we continue to embrace more technology, I think that some people go out of their way to avoid verbal communication. However, certain information can be obtained much more efficiently through a quick call or in-person discussion.

83. WHAT GETS YOU UP IN THE MORNING?

Question Type:

Ambition

Question Analysis:

The interviewer will ask this question to find out what inspires the candidate to work hard every day. Many professionals go through periods of time when they feel unmotivated at work. The interviewer wants to know that the candidate is likely to persist through stressful periods in their career. In your example, you should discuss what inspires you as a professional. It is okay to include inspiration from your personal life (such as "my family") but you should also be sure to discuss inspiration from a professional perspective as well. Great examples include: achieving goals, receiving positive feedback, solving problems, and bringing value to others.

What to Avoid:

You should avoid vague examples such as "my obsession with success" or "my love of the marketing industry." You should also avoid only providing personal inspiration. As mentioned above, it is okay to include something such as "my kids" but you should also include a professional inspiration.

Example Response:

My number one inspiration is to be a great husband to my wife and father to my kids. That motivates me to work hard and succeed as a professional. Throughout my career, I have found motivation in setting challenging goals for myself and working hard to achieve them. I always maintain a running list of short and long-term professional goals and track my progress toward accomplishing them. One of my long-term goals right now is to keep advancing in the finance industry so that I have the opportunity to take on a management role someday.

84. WHAT WAS THE LAST BOOK YOU READ?

Question Type:

Background and Personality

Question Analysis:

The interviewer will use this question to find out more about the candidate's personality and interests outside of work. Your ideal answer is a book related in some way to your profession, even if it is only broadly related, such as a book on leadership. You should never lie to the interviewer in any response, but you can phrase your answer to this question in a way that allows you to discuss a professional book. For example, if the last book you read was "50 Shades of Gray," you can avoid this by saying, "I **recently** read a book called 'From Values to Action' by Harry Kraemer…" Be sure to elaborate on why you liked the book and what you learned from it.

What to Avoid:

Your answer should not be "I don't read outside of work." Even if you need to go back a year or more to the last book you read it is better to mention it than not be able to provide anything. Be sure to refresh yourself on highlights of the book before the interview. You also never want to mention a book you did not actually read. The worst-case scenario is for the interviewer to come back with "I love that book! What was your favorite part?" You will be a deer in the headlights and it will not end well.

Example Response:

I recently read a book called "From Values to Action" by Harry Kraemer. Harry was the former CEO at Baxter, a Fortune 500 healthcare company in the Midwest. In the book Harry argues that some of the strongest results in today's economy are coming from values-based leaders. He discusses the four principals of values-based leadership: Self-reflection, balance, true self-confidence, and genuine humility and how they all come together to guide a leader in their decision making.

I really enjoyed how Harry discussed the ways values can be put into action through his own experiences as a CEO. This book has a lasting message about leading by focusing less on self-advocacy and more on doing the right thing to achieve outstanding results.

85. HOW DO YOU KEEP UP WITH LOCAL NEWS AND WORLD EVENTS?

Question Type:
Background and Personality

Question Analysis:
Employees are not expected to know everything going on in the news, but it is important to keep abreast of the issues that can impact the company, the industry, and its customers. The interviewer will usually ask this question to see if the candidate stays informed or is oblivious to news at the local and world-wide level. Your answer should show that you do put forth an effort to stay informed of local and world-wide news coverage. This could be as simple as checking the news for five minutes each morning before you start your day.

What to Avoid:
You should be careful not to politicize your answer. Today it seems like every news outlet has a perception as being slanted in

a political direction, so it is usually best not to even mention the name of the outlet you typically use to consume the news. For instance, "I watch Fox News every evening after work" or "I read MSNBC.com each morning" can insinuate political leanings and it is smart to avoid this in a professional setting, especially during an interview. However, there are still a few newspapers that are viewed as centered and objective such as The Wall Street Journal and USA Today. It is acceptable to mention a specific news source provided the source is generally viewed as objective.

Example Response:

Before I start work, I like to log on to my computer and take five to ten minutes to read the news headlines for the day. If I come across news that could have an impact on the company or industry, I will take the time to read it and consider its significance. I also like to watch the local news in the evening to keep informed of the events going on in the local community.

86. DO YOU SEEK OUT TRAINING AND CONTINUING EDUCATION?

Question Type:

Industry and Company Specific

Question Analysis:

In most professional positions, success requires constantly evolving skills and knowledge. Continuing professional education is highly important and valuable to most companies.

Additionally, continuing education is often required for those who maintain a professional license or certification. The interviewer will use this question to see if the candidate has the initiative and desire to continue learning new skills within their profession. You should discuss your interest in continuing education and provide examples of participating in trainings or conferences in the past.

What to Avoid:

You should avoid telling the interviewer that you have not had the opportunity to pursue continuing education. Even if your previous employer did not offer training, you can still discuss utilizing free online resources or publications to keep up with your industry and learn new skills.

Example Response:

Continuing my education in the digital marketing industry and learning new skills that can bring value to my employer and career are very important to me. In my previous position, I had the opportunity to attend training seminars each quarter that included design thinking exercises as well as presentations from some of the top thought leaders in the industry. I also subscribe to the Journal of Digital and Social Media Marketing and frequently seek out online trainings and courses.

87. IN ONE SENTENCE, HOW WOULD YOU DESCRIBE THE INTERNET TO SOMEONE FROM THE 1800'S?

Question Type:

Communication

Question Analysis:

Candidates often freeze up for these types of questions because they are difficult to anticipate and seem somewhat random. The interviewer will use this type of question to assess how well the candidate can take something complex and simplify it. They will also use the question to see how well the candidate can think on the spot and follow instructions. When condensing something complex, you should focus your answer on the "what" and "why" components of the topic.

What to Avoid:

You should always abide by the rules of the question (in this case keeping it to one sentence) and avoid long run on sentences. Remember that your task is to simply describe something from a high level. Your answer should not go into the granular details of the topic.

Example Response:

Think of the internet as a railroad with the tracks as networks, and the trains containing information. The internet is used to transmit information across the globe the way railroads can carry people or cargo to different destinations across the country.

88. WHEN WOULD YOU BE ABLE TO START?

Question Type:

Background and Personality

Question Analysis:

Candidates often interpret this question as a job offer and blurt out an overly-excited response. However, it is not uncommon for interviewers to ask all candidates this question during the interview to ensure there will not be any restrictions or long-term delays to a start date if there ends up being an offer. Your answer should demonstrate your willingness to be flexible, but you should be honest about any limitations.

What to Avoid:

Your answer should not make you sound too excited or desperate. "Right now!" would sound impulsive and be a big turnoff to the interviewer. You should also not make any promises that you cannot keep. It is okay if you need to fulfill an obligation with a previous employer before starting the new job. Just be upfront and honest about it with the interviewer.

Example Response:

My current employer's policy calls for a three weeks advanced notice before leaving the company. I plan to honor that commitment so if I was offered the position, I would just need the three weeks to wrap up at my current job. Aside from that, I am flexible with the start date.

89. IF YOU WERE THE OWNER OF A COMPANY, WHAT WOULD YOU SELECT FOR ITS TOP THREE VALUES?

Question Type:
Background and Personality

Question Analysis:
The interviewer will use this question to assess how well the candidate's values would fit in with the company's culture. Researching the company's values and culture prior to the interview will help you focus on your values that have strong overlap with the company.

What to Avoid:
You should avoid discussing values that are not relevant to the company's business. For example, "produce social value" would be a great value when interviewing for an online advertising position but it is probably not relevant for a role in finance. You should also not use the company's values verbatim. It is beneficial to have some overlap when elaborating on your values, but it will be perceived as disingenuous by the interviewer if you respond with the exact values found on the company's website.

Example Response:
If I owned a business, my top three values would be: integrity, quality, and innovation. I believe that integrity is an essential component for building strong relationships with team

members and customers. When a company commits to quality they are demonstrating pride in their work and establishing a lasting reputation. Having an environment that fosters innovation encourages creativity and leads to better ideas, processes, and products.

90. DO YOU VOLUNTEER YOUR TIME IN THE LOCAL COMMUNITY?

Question Type:

Background and Personality

Question Analysis:

Most companies take the initiative to give back to their local communities. They will often encourage employees to participate in company sponsored fundraising or volunteer activities. The interviewer will use this question to find out if the candidate is likely to participate in volunteer events. They may also use the question to see if the candidate participates in productive activities outside of work. It is okay if you are not actively involved in a volunteer role. You can still talk about past volunteer events and discuss local organizations or volunteer opportunities that have sparked your interest. A great way to end your response to this question is to ask the interviewer about how the company encourages volunteering.

What to Avoid:

Even if you have not volunteered your time, you should avoid a simple "no, I have not" response. Instead, focus your answer on local organizations or volunteer opportunities that you have considered and discuss your desire to take the next steps.

Example Response:

Giving back to the local community is important to me. Since moving here last year, I have not had the opportunity to get involved with a charitable organization yet, but I have started to look into opportunities with the local Habitat for Humanity chapter. When I lived in XYZ City, I enjoyed volunteering with this organization often. Does XYZ Company offer volunteer opportunities to its employees?

91. WHERE DO YOU SEE YOURSELF IN TEN YEARS?

Question Type:

Ambition

Question Analysis:

When the interviewer asks about your goals ten years in advance, they are usually looking for information beyond just the commitment to the company and profession. They are typically trying to ascertain your desire to work towards management or executive leadership roles. They will also use the question to ensure you are not unrealistic in your ambitions. In your response, you should demonstrate eagerness to grow within the company but avoid over-ambitious responses such as "I will be CEO of the company."

What to Avoid:

Unless you are interviewing at a small company where you will only be a promotion or two away from an executive role, you should avoid specific job titles in your response such as "CFO" or "CEO." With too many unknown variables over a ten-year span, it will sound unrealistic. On the other end of the spectrum, you should avoid sounding content with settling into your role for the long-term. You can express your desire to advance within the company and seize opportunities while at the same time not mentioning specific job titles.

Example Response:

There are many unknown variables over ten years, but I am committed to learning as much as I can in each opportunity that comes up in my career. I believe that my work ethic and eagerness to grow as an individual and within a team will bring value to this company in any role. Over the next ten years, I plan to set ambitious but attainable goals to establish myself as a key resource and leader within the company.

92. IF YOU WERE AN ANIMAL, WHAT WOULD YOU BE AND WHY?

Question Type:

Background and Personality

Question Analysis:

This can seem like an oddball question, but some interviewers will ask it to find out how well the candidate thinks on the spot since most people will not prepare for this type of question. There is no need to overthink this question or get philosophical with your response. You should keep your answer simple and it should be an animal with a positive reputation. Your answer should include positive traits of the animal that are desired in a professional setting.

What to Avoid:

There are a lot of good possible answers here, but you should avoid choosing animals with bad reputations such as snakes or rats. You should also avoid discussing traits that are not relevant to the professional setting such as "a shark because I am a fast swimmer."

Example Response:

I would be a dog because I am attentive, loyal, reliable, and offer support to those who need it.

93. IN YOUR ESTIMATION, HOW MANY GAS STATIONS ARE THERE IN THE UNITED STATES?

Question Type:
Critical Thinking

Question Analysis:
The logic and estimates are pretty straight forward in question #61 but this question seems much more complicated. It is important to remember not to panic over a question like this. It is okay if you have no clue on the inputs, just ask yourself what

data would you would need to come to an answer and then focus your response on the logic and thought process.

What to Avoid:

Even when you have no idea about the specific numbers or data to use for a question like this, it is important to avoid a random guess. A response such as "I have no idea, but I'll guess 100,0000" would convey weak problem-solving capabilities to the interviewer.

Example Response:

I am going to go out on a limb here and estimate that there is an average of 300 municipalities in each state for a total of 15,000 (300 x 50 states). I would then estimate that there is an average of 3 gas stations per municipality for a total of 45,000 gas stations in the U.S. Of course, if I had my computer in front of me I would be able to avoid estimates and use more accurate data to come to my conclusion.

94. HOW MANY HOURS DO YOU TYPICALLY WORK PER WEEK?

Question Type:

Background and Personality

Question Analysis:

This can be a tricky question because the interviewer is typically not necessarily looking for a specific number of hours. Instead, they are using the question to find out if the candidate's mindset is to work a fixed number of hours or if they are willing to work the number of hours it takes to get the job done. That can mean working 40 hours some weeks and beyond 40 hours others. If you do work a fixed number of hours, your answer should demonstrate that you are willing to work the hours needed to accomplish the job.

What to Avoid:

Unless the interviewer insists on it, you should avoid a fixed number in your response. You should also avoid an unnecessary and impractical response such as "I'm willing to work 100 hours every week."

Example Response:

Our department tends to get very busy toward the end of the calendar year so the number of hours I work per week can fluctuate depending on our workload and deadlines. Some weeks I am able to get through my work in 40 hours but other weeks I work closer to 60 hours to ensure we meet our client's needs and project deadlines. I am a firm believer in focusing less on a certain number of hours and more on doing what it takes to get the job done. With that said, I also try to find a good work-life balance.

95. IN YOUR ESTIMATION, HOW MANY TIMES HEAVIER IS AN ELEPHANT THAN A MOUSE?

Question Type:

Critical Thinking

Question Analysis:

Unless you are interviewing for an engineering position or another highly technical role, the interviewer will typically not hit you with complex math questions. However, it is not uncommon to be asked a mathematical question like this to assess your analytical thought process. There is obviously not an exact answer the interviewer is looking for here. The key to a successful response is to walk them through your thought process and deliver a logical guess.

What to Avoid:

No matter how ridiculous the question sounds, you should never get flustered and respond with something such as "Ohh boy, I have no idea." If you get caught off guard with a question like this, take your time and think through a response. You should also never provide a guess here without the reasoning. Even if you had logical reasoning behind your guess, the interviewer will not know that unless you talk them through your thought process.

Example Response:

Well, I am going to go out on a limb and guess that an average mouse weighs one-tenth of a pound and an average elephant weighs 10,000 pounds so my estimate is 100,000 times heavier.

96. WOULD YOU BE WILLING TO RELOCATE DOWN THE ROAD IF NEEDED?

Question Type:

Background and Personality

Question Analysis:

This question can catch many candidates off guard because it sounds as if there may already be a plan in place to relocate the position. However, unless the job description explicitly states that there may be a move required, the interviewer is typically using this question just to gauge the candidate's enthusiasm for the company and position. Your answer should emphasize your enthusiasm for the position while being honest about your willingness to relocate. Remember, the chances of actually being asked to relocate are usually slim unless the interviewer explicitly discusses a plan already in place. If you would like to know if there is a relocation plan in place, you can ask the question at the end of your response.

What to Avoid:

You typically want to avoid an oversimplified "yes" or "no" response to this question. If you are not willing to relocate, you can mention that it may be something you are open to in the future. If you are willing to relocate, you should emphasize your enthusiasm for the opportunity over a simple "yes." Be sure to avoid responses that sound self-serving such as "if relocating paid more money" or "if I was relocated to a nice area."

Example Response, Willing to Relocate:
I am excited about the opportunity this position offers and would be willing to relocate if needed. Is there currently a plan in place to relocate this position down the road?

Example Response, Not Ready to Relocate:
I am excited about the opportunity this position offers. Right now, I am not able to relocate but would be open to the idea in the future.

97. HOW WOULD YOU DESCRIBE THE PACE AT WHICH YOU WORK?

Question Type:
Background and Personality

Question Analysis:
"Fast" is usually the first word that comes to mind for most candidates when considering a response to this question. It is true that employers seek efficient workers, but a response that only underlines speedy work can give the interviewer cause for concern about quality. Interviewers are looking for a response that demonstrates efficiency but also emphasizes work which is based on thoughtfulness and careful consideration.

What to Avoid:
You should avoid oversimplified answers such as "lightening fast." Instead, show that you care about efficiency but are also methodical when completing your work.

Example Response:

I am a steady worker who takes prides in getting my work done in an efficient manner, but I never sacrifice quality for speed. There are circumstances that require careful planning and consideration before the execution and I have no problem taking my time to ensure the work is done right.

98. KIM'S MOTHER HAD FOUR CHILDREN. THE FIRST CHILD WAS NAMED APRIL, THE SECOND WAS NAMED MAY, AND THE THIRD JUNE. WHAT WAS THE NAME OF THE FOURTH CHILD?

Question Type:
Critical Thinking

Question Analysis:
This is a trick question that requires the candidate to rely on listening and critical thinking skills to come to the right answer. Candidates often jump to a quick answer instead of comprehending the whole question and thinking it through. Remember, the answer for a trick question is not usually difficult, but it is not usually obvious either. If the interviewer asks you a question like this, be sure to take your time and think through the question before responding.

What to Avoid:
You should avoid a quick and impulsive response to these

questions. You want to show the interviewer that you can listen and analyze information before acting.

Example Response:

The question said, "Kim's mother" so if the other three children were named April, May, and June, the fourth child must be named Kim.

99. WHAT HAS BEEN YOUR MOST MEMORABLE REGRET IN LIFE?

Question Type:

Background and Personality

Question Analysis:

The interviewer will use this question to get a better sense of the candidate's character and personality. You should be careful not to get caught up in the dramatic tone of this question. The interviewer is not looking for you to tell them about past relationships or anything else that is too personal. You should try to discuss a regret connected in some way to your education or career. A great answer will demonstrate accountability and finish with the lessons learned.

What to Avoid:

A common response to this question is "I have no regrets in life," but the interviewer knows this is not true, so you should avoid this answer. You should also avoid excuses and blame placed on others when explaining your regret.

Example Response:

In a prior position as a systems analyst, my manager informed me that there was an immediate need for help on the IT team at our Japan location. He asked if I would be interested in relocating on a one-year assignment, but he needed an answer shortly. The timing was not ideal as my wife and I had just closed on our first home and she had recently started a new job. However, she was supportive and on board with the move if we felt it was the right thing to do for my career.

After a long weekend of us both changing our minds many times, we ultimately declined the offer to relocate. Looking back on it, we both agree it was the wrong decision. The opportunity to work closely with senior management in a rapidly growing business unit would have been invaluable to my career. We also would have had the incredible experience to live a full year in a different environment and culture. I have learned that when big opportunities come up, it is important to take advantage of them and not worry too much about the small stuff. After volunteering my name for future travel opportunities within the company, my manager assigned me to multiple global projects which gave me the chance to travel and partner with our foreign business units.

100. DO YOU HAVE ANY QUESTIONS FOR ME?

Question Analysis:

Although this question is covered in tip #2, it is worth emphasizing that asking the interviewer well thought out and relevant questions is one of the most important aspects of the interview. The questions will tell the interviewer a lot about your interest and enthusiasm in the company and whether you came prepared for the interview. Most of your questions should be specific to the interviewer or company and be open-ended to promote discussion.

What to Avoid:

You should avoid asking overly generic questions that are not tailored toward either the interviewer, company, or position. For example, a question such as "Who are the company's top competitors?" says to the interviewer that you did not do much research before the interview whereas "What are the most significant challenges when forecasting sales for seasonally driven products?" shows you came in with a strong understanding of the position, company, and industry.

Example Questions:

When you transitioned into a leadership role in the engineering group, what measures did you take to promote team collaboration?

What would you say are the top reasons this company has been able to sustain double-digit growth over the past few years?

In what ways will the technical teams support this sales position when working with customers to find solutions for their network infrastructure challenges?

Since this position requires an active CPA license, how does the company support employees who are required to obtain a set amount of continuing education credits each year?

This company has been consistently ranked as a top place to work in the area for many years. If the employees were polled, what would be their top reasons for voting this company as a great place to work?

APPENDIX: VIRTUAL AND PHONE INTERVIEWS

Companies will often use virtual or phone interviews to screen applicants before they extend them an invite to interview on-site. However, some companies will conduct the full interview process virtually. Especially if the interview is for a "work-at-home" position.

The virtual interview is also frequently used to dwindle down a large group of candidates into a manageable size for the in-person interviews.

Most of the information in this book is still highly relevant for the virtual interview process, but there are five additional tips below which are specific to the process and can be beneficial to the success of your next virtual or phone interview.

1. ALWAYS BE PREPARED

Companies will often reach out to applicants to thank them for applying, ask them a couple questions, and schedule a follow up virtual or onsite interview. Most candidates think the interview starts at that next appointment, but the truth is it already started with the call. It may not sound official or represent an interview, but companies like to use all instances of communication to assess the candidate. This means that you

196

should treat all communication with the company as if you were sitting down in an official interview.

2. ENSURE THERE WILL BE NO TECHNICAL ISSUES

<u>Phone Interviews:</u> Be sure to use a reliable phone. If you will be using a mobile device, be sure to interview in a location with excellent service and make sure the battery has enough power to last at least 30 minutes beyond the planned duration of the interview. I recommend having quick access to a charger and electrical outlet in the event that the interview goes longer than expected and your battery gets low.

<u>Virtual Interviews:</u> You should get comfortable with the software in advance and ensure it works properly. For example, if your virtual interview will be on Zoom, you should setup a practice Zoom meeting with a friend or family member. On the practice meeting, you can ensure the software is working correctly on your computer (be sure to use a device with a working camera) and familiarize yourself with the features. When it comes time for the interview, you want to feel comfortable and confident with the software. If you start having technical issues during your live interview, it can be very distracting and hurt your chances.

You should also plan to use a reliable internet connection. Most smart phones today have "hotspots" that allow you to connect a computer to the phone's network. I recommend trying this out and using it as an emergency backup if your internet connection goes out during your interview.

3. BE MINDFUL NOT TO INTERRUPT THE INTERVIEWER

For phone interviews, not having eye contact and verbal cues, can make it difficult to avoid interrupting the other person on the line. To avoid interrupting the interviewer, be sure to wait an extra second after they pause or ask a question, to ensure they have completed their line of dialogue.

4. USE A RELIABLY QUIET SPACE

Coffee shops and other public places make for horrible places to do virtual interviews for many obvious reasons. If you plan to do the interview from home, be sure your spouse or roommates will be aware of the situation. Any type of background noises can ruin the interview.

5. DO NOT OVER RELY ON CHEAT SHEETS

It can be beneficial to have some notes in front of you to quickly reference when needed but you should avoid trying to rely on them to get you through the interview. If you have a stack of papers you plan to use, it will be obvious to the interviewer when they hear or see you flipping through them to find your answer. When candidates place a heavy reliance on notes they also tend to come into the interview under prepared.

CLOSING THOUGHTS

I want to thank you for reading this book and wish you all the best in your interviews!

If you have any questions about the material or just want to reach out to connect, feel free to send me an email: matt@encoursa.com. I would also greatly appreciate you taking a minute to leave me feedback on this book.

To Your Success!

Matthew Briggson